CHRISTIAN MONASTICISM IN EGYPT

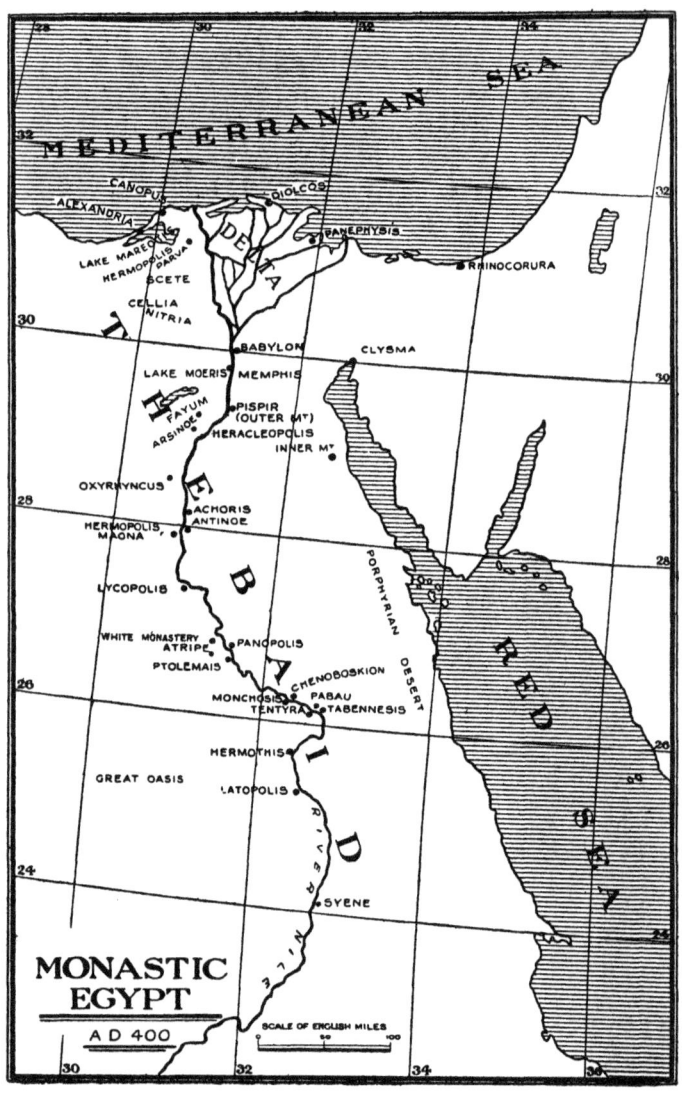

STUDIES IN CHURCH HISTORY

Christian Monasticism in Egypt

TO THE CLOSE OF THE FOURTH CENTURY

BY THE REV.
W. H. MACKEAN, D.D.

WIPF & STOCK · Eugene, Oregon

Wipf and Stock Publishers
199 W 8th Ave, Suite 3
Eugene, OR 97401

Christian Monasticism in Egypt
To the Close of the Fourth Century
By Mackean, W. H.
Softcover ISBN-13: 978-1-6667-3624-3
Hardcover ISBN-13: 978-1-6667-9430-4
eBook ISBN-13: 978-1-6667-9431-1
Publication date 11/1/2021
Previously published by SPCK, 1920

This edition is a scanned facsimile of
the original edition published in 1920.

CONTENTS

MAP		*Frontispiece*
		PAGE
PREFACE		7
PRINCIPAL SOURCES FOR EGYPTIAN MONASTICISM (FOURTH CENTURY)		9
ABBREVIATIONS		11
I CHRISTIAN MONASTICISM AND NON-CHRISTIAN ASCETIC SYSTEMS		13
1. INDIAN		14
2. GREEK		17
3. EGYPTIAN		18
4. JEWISH		22
II. THE ORIGIN OF CHRISTIAN MONASTICISM IN EGYPT		25
1. ASCETICISM IN EGYPT		26
A NON-CHRISTIAN		26
B CHRISTIAN		36
2. MYSTICISM IN EGYPT		53
3. EGYPTIAN BELIEF IN A FUTURE LIFE		57
4. CIRCUMSTANCES OF THE EGYPTIAN CHURCH		60
5. CONDITION OF EGYPT		63
6. TENDENCY IN EGYPT TOWARDS THE DESERT		66
7. EXAMPLE OF S. ANTHONY		69
III. TYPES OF EGYPTIAN MONASTICISM		76
1. EREMITICAL MONASTICISM		77
2. ASSOCIATIONS OF EREMITES		78
i. PISPIR		79
ii. CHENOBOSKION (SCHENESIT)		80
iii. NITRIA		81
iv. CELLIA		84
v. SCETE		86
vi. VARIOUS ASSOCIATIONS, ETC.		88

Contents

III. Types of Egyptian Monasticism (cont.)

    3. Cenobitic Monasticism 91
        i. Community of Aotas 91
        ii. Pachomian System 91
        iii. White Monastery 110
        iv. Other Cenobitic Monasteries . . . 113
        v. Communities of Women 118

IV. Aspects of Egyptian Monasticism . . . 121

    1. Sacrifices of the Monks . . . 121
    2. Social and Intellectual Status of the Monks 125
    3. Monasticism and the Church . . 128
    4. Peaceful Simplicity of the Monastic Life and its Interruptions 134

V. Spread of Egyptian Monasticism . . . 140

    1. Pilgrimages to Egypt 141
    2. Work of Athanasius 147

Conclusion 152

Index 154

PREFACE

ALTHOUGH various books and articles have been published recently upon the subject of monasticism, there is singularly little that deals with its origin in Egypt. English, French and German writers, whose works cover a wider field, have necessarily been unable to devote much space to the particular question of the origin. The purpose therefore of the first part of this study is an attempt to show how monasticism grew out of the special conditions of thought and life in Egypt, a mode of approach which has not apparently been adopted elsewhere to the same extent.

The latter part deals with a subject that has been treated attractively by many writers, but it aims at being a survey of the first century of monasticism in Egypt, based upon those sources which have been generally accepted by recent criticism as the most reliable.

It includes, too, a detailed account of the Pachomian system, derived mainly from the Greek life of Pachomius and the Latin Rules of Jerome, for the additional reason that the subject has not been treated at any length by English writers. Moreover, P. Ladeuze in his great work was preoccupied with demonstrating the superiority of the Greek to the Coptic and Arabic versions of the life of Pachomius, and with refuting the views of Amélineau and Grützmacher.

I have made also considerable use of Cassian's works,

not only for the thought which inspired the monks, and for details of the eremitical life, but for the growth of cenobitic monasticism, apart from the Pachomian system. For little attention has been paid to such institutions mentioned by him as well as the author of *Historia Monachorum* and Jerome; and yet Cassian's many references to that form of monasticism were not as a rule (except *Instit.*, iv. 1–18) made to the Pachomian communities, which he had not visited.

Special attention also is devoted to the place and work of Athanasius in the cause of monasticism, as regards both its relation to the Egyptian Church and its spread in various countries of the West.

It remains to be added that no modern writer on the subject can fail to be under great obligations to C. Butler for his edition of the Lausiac History, and to P. Ladeuze for his *Étude sur le Cénobitisme Pakhomien*. I hope that I have expressed my indebtedness to other writers, from whom I have learned much; and I am conscious of the influence of Dr. H. B. Workman's excellent treatise on *The Evolution of the Monastic Ideal*.

My grateful thanks are due to Canon A. C. Headlam, Regius Professor of Divinity at Oxford, for various criticisms and suggestions; and I am specially indebted to my wife for help in preparing this little work for publication.

PRINCIPAL SOURCES FOR EGYPTIAN MONASTICISM

(FOURTH CENTURY)

GENERAL.

Athanasius, *Vita Antonii*. Migne, *P.G.* 26, p. 835 ff. (E.T., Nicene and post-Nicene Fathers.)

Palladius, *Historia Lausiaca*. Texts and Studies, vi. 2, E. C. Butler. (E.T., W. K. L. Clarke ; Translations of Christian Literature.)

Historia Monachorum in Aegypto, Palladius und Rufinus. E. Preuschen.

Cassian, *De Institutis Coenobiorum : Collationes*. Corpus Script. Eccl , Latin., Petschenig. (E.T., Nicene and post-Nicene Fathers)

Sozomen, *Historia Ecclesiastica* (especially vi. 32–4). Migne, *P.G.* 67. (E.T., Nicene and post-Nicene Fathers.)

Sulpitius Severus, *Dialogus* I. Corpus Script. Eccl , Latin., Halm. (E.T., Nicene and post-Nicene Fathers.)

PACHOMIAN MONASTICISM.

Vita Pachomii. (Greek.) *Acta Sanctorum*, Maii., t. iii. Append., p. 22 f

(Bohairic.) *Annales du Musée Guimet*, xvii. p. 1 ff.

(Sahidic Fragments.) *Annales du Musée Guimet*, xvii. p. 295 ff. *Mission Archéologique française au Caire ;* E. Amélineau, *Monuments pour servir à l'hist. de l'Egypte chrétienne*, t. 4, ii. 521–608.

10 Principal Sources for Egyptian Monasticism

Opera Pachomii, etc. (Coptic Fragments.) Zoega, *Catalogus codicum Coptic.*, 168, 169, 174, 176. E. Amélineau, op. cit., t. 4, ii.

Epistolæ Pachomii. Migne, *P.L.* 23, p. 87 ff.

Regulæ Pachomii (Latin Transl. by Jerome). Migne, *P.L.* 23, p. 61 ff.

Epistola Ammonis. *Acta Sanctorum*, Maii, t. iii. Append , p. 54 ff.

Doctrina de Institutione Monachorum (Orsisius). Migne, *P.L.* 103, p. 453 ff.

WHITE MONASTERY.

Schenoudi. (Bohairic Life.) E. Amélineau, op. cit., t. 4 (i.) pp. 1–91. (Coptic Fragments.) E. Amélineau, op. cit., t. 4 (i.) 229–46, 277–87 ; (ii) 633–49. Zoega, op. cit., 212, 230. Cf. Leipoldt, *Schenute von Atripe.*

The value of the sources and texts for Egyptian monasticism has been fully discussed by E. Amélineau (*Annales du Musée Guimet*, xvii.), G. Grutzmacher (*Pachomius und das älteste Klosterleben*), E. Preuschen (*Palladius und Rufinus*), O. Zöckler (*Askese und Mönchtum*), C. Butler, P. Ladeuze, S. Schiwietz (*Das morgenlandische Monchtum*), and a convenient summary is given by H. B. Workman (*The Evolution of the Monastic Ideal*), p 353 ff.

ABBREVIATIONS

Annales	*Annales du Musée Guimet*, xvii.
C. Butler.	*Historia Lausiaca of Palladius.* Texts and Studies, vi.
Coll.	*Collationes* (Cassian).
E.R.E.	*Encyclopædia of Religion and Ethics* (Hastings).
Harnack, *H.D.*	*History of Dogma*
Harnack, *M.E C.*	*Mission and Expansion of Christianity.*
H.D.B.	Hastings, *Dictionary of the Bible.*
H.L.	*Historia Lausiaca.*
H M.	*Historia Monachorum in Aegypto.*
Instit	*De Institutis* (Cassian).
Ital. Sacr.	*Italia Sacra*, F. Ughelli.
J.T.S	*Journal of Theological Studies*
Ladeuze.	P. Ladeuze, *Étude sur le Cénobitisme Pakhomien.*
M.	*Mission Archéologique Française au Caire*, E. Amélineau. *Monuments pour servir à l'hist. de l'Egypte chrétienne*, t. 4.
Reg.	*Regulæ Pachomii* (Jerome).
Zoega.	*Catalogus codicum Copticorum.*

CHRISTIAN MONASTICISM IN EGYPT

I

CHRISTIAN MONASTICISM AND NON-CHRISTIAN
ASCETIC SYSTEMS

MONASTICISM, or Monachism, properly denotes the life of lonely isolation, " a system of living which owes its origin to those tendencies of the human soul which are summed up in the words asceticism and mysticism."[1] At first the word was applied to the eremitical mode of life, but it came generally to denote the cenobitic life, or the organisation of the ascetic life on a social basis. Therefore in its widest signification it denoted the life which ascetics lived apart from the world, whether in solitary isolation or in common with others like-minded. The problem which confronts the student of early Christian monasticism is the cause of its rise at the beginning of the fourth century in the eremitical form which rapidly developed into the cenobitic life. Now monasticism was not confined to the Christian Church, for it was found in highly organised forms before the Christian era. The question therefore that arises is

[1] *Encycl. Brit.*, 11th ed , xviii. p. 687.

whether the origin of Christian monasticism is to be sought in an Egyptian institution or in non-Christian ascetic systems among the Indians, Greeks, or Jews, where we find many for various reasons and in different ages despising the world and its pleasures, forsaking the haunts of man and retiring to solitude, where they fasted, meditated and devoted themselves to a celibate life.

1. *Indian.*

In Buddhism, A. Hilgenfeld[1] found the origin of Christian monasticism. Moreover, in recent years the traces of Indian thought have been frequently sought in early Christian literature; and W. M. F. Petrie[2] has emphasised the influence of India upon ascetic developments in Egypt. But the search for such influence is a singularly elusive and obscure process; and, so far as Christian monasticism is concerned, there are adequate reasons for rejecting such a theory.

1. Although there is a certain superficial resemblance between Buddhist and Christian monasticism, as indeed there must be in all ascetic systems, the contrast is great. According to Buddhist teaching, salvation could be found only in monasticism. The Buddhist worked at no trade and despised manual labour, which was left to the novices; the Christian devoted much time to working with his hands, and the cenobitic life was organised on an industrial basis. Moreover, the Christian lived by the proceeds of his labours, but the Buddhist depended upon mendicancy. The former ate no meat, the latter only abstained if he were adopting a stricter asceticism for

[1] *Zeitschr f Wissenschaft Theol*, 1878, pp. 148 ff.
[2] *Personal Religion in Egypt*, pp. 62 ff.

Non-Christian Ascetic Systems 15

a limited period. The Buddhist had no acts of worship similar to Christian gatherings for the offices. The Indian orders were loosely organised, and their monks displayed a characteristic independence in wandering where they would.

2. In India, the eremitical life developed into the life of a community, as was the case in the Christian monasticism of Egypt If, then, Christian monasticism was an imitation of Indian monasticism, we should expect it to have started with the cenobitic life ; but the evidence of history is to the contrary. Both showed a similar development from the eremitical to the cenobitic life.

3. It is impossible to trace any direct connection between them Excavations by the British School of Archæology in Egypt have revealed traces of Indian influence, dating probably from the fifth century B.C., in the period when the Persian domination included both Egypt and India. For in the foreign quarter of Memphis there have been discovered small heads in pottery of the various races that gathered there. Besides a figure of a Tibetan Mongolian, there are represented an Aryan woman of the Punjab and a seated figure in Indian attitude. The date given to the Indian woman by W. M. F. Petrie is c 200 B.C.[1] Further, about 259 B.C., Asoka, Emperor of India, determined to spread the teaching of Buddhism in distant lands, and amongst the countries on the Mediterranean to which he sent Buddhist missionaries was Egypt during the reign of Ptolemy Philadelphus.[2] But apparently they were not successful in founding any Buddhist organisation.

[1] *Man*, VIII. 71.
[2] V. A. Smith, *Asoka*, p. 42 f.

Mention, however, may be made of the Egyptian Gymnosophists, whom Apollonius of Tyana[1] was represented to have found in Ethiopia. They lived on rising ground not far from the Nile, and existed in the open air, having neither huts nor houses. Their places of worship were scattered here and there on the hill, and a small portico was built for strangers. They ate no animal food, and a dinner, consisting of vegetables, bread and sweatmeats, was provided for their visitors Their general meetings were held in a small park, where the business of the community was transacted. The head was named Thespesion. A tradition existed that the origin of this mode of life was Indian, but they resented the idea of such connection. It is, however, difficult to say how much importance should be attached to this account ; but even if it be accepted as wholly historical, it indicates simply the existence of an isolated and distant community of ascetics in the first century A.D., who may have been descendants of the Buddhist mission, but were probably little known, and had no connection with the Christian monasticism of more than two hundred years afterwards. The utmost influence of such a community would have been to make a slight contribution to the prevalent tendency towards asceticism in Egypt.

The link between Egypt and India was commercial. The trade between Alexandria and India, which led writers to take more interest in that distant land, was at its height at the end of the second and the beginning of the third century. Afterwards a gradual decline of the trade set in, and by the year 275 " it was in so languishing a state that in so far as that it was a trade directed and controlled by Alexandrian merchants, it

[1] *Vit.*, vi. 6 ff.

may almost be said to have died out."[1] Consequently the Alexandrian interest in India seems to have disappeared many years before the arrival of monasticism, although it is quite possible that a few Indians may have still been found in the cosmopolitan city of Alexandria, as was the case in the time of Dion Chrysostom.[2] But the barrier of race no doubt prevented a close contact with the inhabitants, and the difficulty of language would also to some extent have stood in the way, even if such traders had been filled with missionary zeal.

As to the connection between India and Christianity in Egypt, it may be said that very little was known of India and its religions by Christian writers; the name of Buddha stands as a phantom in their pages; their information was mainly derived from older writers; those who were so interested in India[3] belonged to a period previous to the rise of Christian monasticism, and their interest was the result of the Empire's commerce with a distant and mysterious land. If that be the case at Alexandria, it is still less probable that the Copts were affected by the religious thought and practices of India.

2. *Greek.*

Asceticism was a characteristic mark of the Orphic and Pythagorean systems, but no connection can be established between them and Coptic monasticism.[4]

Neo-Platonism, however, represented an important development of Greek asceticism at Alexandria in the

[1] *The Indian Travels of Apollonius of Tyana, and the Indian Embassies to Rome*, O. de B. Priaulx, p. 163.
[2] *Orat.*, xxxi. p. 672, Reske.
[3] Clement, *Strom.*, i. 15; iii. 7; Origen, *c. Cels.*, i. 12, 24.
[4] See also *E.R.E.*, viii. p. 782.

third and fourth centuries A.D. It differed from early forms of philosophy, by emphasising the contemplative instead of the practical side of life ; and its followers held that if the soul was purified from all earthly thoughts it could attain to the contemplation of God. This freedom from material interests was to be sought by isolation and asceticism. Thus we have in neo-Platonism the tendency to withdraw from the world coupled with an ascetic and contemplative life, which are the characteristics of monasticism. But the origin of the latter cannot be found therein for the following reasons —

i. Although this philosophy was eagerly followed by the thoughtful of the third and fourth centuries, and deeply influenced Christian thought, yet its appeal was to the few, and only to those of Hellenic education. Monasticism, on the other hand, was originally a Coptic movement, adopted by men often ignorant of Greek ; and it is impossible to suppose that the rural population of the Thebaid was so affected by neo-Platonic thought as to inaugurate the monastic movement.

ii. "It appears to have remained a purely personal matter, and not to have led to the practice of the eremitical life or the formation of religious communities."[1]

3. *Egyptian.*

H. Weingarten over forty years ago was responsible for the theory that the origin of Christian monasticism was to be found in Egyptian paganism. As, however, this belief still survives,[2] it may be worth while to investigate the subject.

[1] C. Butler, i. p. 229.
[2] e.g. T. R. Glover, *The Conflict of Religions in the Early Roman Empire*, p. 24.

Non-Christian Ascetic Systems

References have been found in fragments of papyri[1] to certain recluses who were consecrated to the cult of Serapis, of whom the chief was Ptolemy, son of Glaucias, of Macedonian origin, at Memphis (c. 165 B.C.). There is mention also of Apollonius, brother of Ptolemy, and Thaues and Taous. The two latter were priestesses, who were known by the official title of "the twins," probably because twin sisters were originally chosen for the purpose. Ptolemy had been the friend of their dead father; he got them this position and acted as their protector. They appear to have been possessed of little learning; they lived in the temple, brought to Serapis the gifts that were made for the welfare of the Royal family, and took part in the funeral ceremonies for the dead Apis. In this way they obtained a home and an income, received in kind, of bread, oil and flax. These recluses were of indigenous origin and known by the name of κάτοχοι, which means "possessed of Serapis"; and, as E. Preuschen[2] has shown, there is no evidence at all to support the interpretation of "enclosed," which was suggested by C. J C Reuvens.[3] They appear to have been very few in number, lived in the temple or a dependent building for varying periods, which they could terminate when they pleased, and were allowed some intercourse with the outside world, but they were not permitted to leave the temple precincts. They came for various reasons, to obtain a cure, or an oracle by the rite of incubation, for Serapis was a god of healing, often identified with Aesculapius, and many of the

---

[1] Acad. des Inscript. et belles-lettres, *mem. présent. par divers savants*, 1st series, ii. 1852, pp 552 ff , *Bibliothèque Impériale, notices et extraits des mss* , t 18, 1858, pp 261 ff.
[2] *Mönchthum und Serapiskult*, p. 27 f
[3] *Lettres à M. Letronne sur les pap. biling. et grecs*, 1830, pp. 84 ff

Serapis inscriptions are thanksgivings for restoration to health. Some exercised priestly functions; and they appear to have been the medium of those seeking revelations, and were consequently found in the most frequented temples. They were very poor, called themselves beggars, and were often complaining of their condition.

But their aim and mode of life were clearly different from those of the Christian monk; they were not celibates, nor were they characterised by religious fervour; they were not penitents strictly enclosed, as Weingarten alleges; the poverty of which they complain bears no resemblance to the asceticism of the monks, nor was the earliest monasticism found in an enclosure. Moreover, there is no support whatever from the records of monasticism for such a theory; indeed, the general attitude of Christian monks was very antagonistic to paganism.

There is, however, one point that requires special consideration, for E. Revillout,[1] G. Grützmacher[2] and others have tried to maintain that Pachomius, the founder of Egyptian cenobitism, was a monk of Serapis. The problem centres round the time that Pachomius spent at Chenoboskion (or Schenesit) in the Southern Thebaid after he had left the army. There, according to the Greek account,[3] after receiving the first elements of the Christian faith, he was baptised, and received a vision concerning his future mission. Then, moved by the Spirit of God, he wished to become a monk, and sought out the anchorite Palæmon, of whom he had heard.

[1] *Révue Egyptol.*, 1880, p 160.
[2] *Pachomius und das älteste Klosterleben*, pp. 39 ff.
[3] *Vit. Pach.*, 3 f

The Bohairic and Arabic accounts,[1] however, add that Pachomius, choosing Schenesit because only a few people lived there, went to the river bank and found a small temple, named by the ancients a temple of Serapis. There he prayed, and, moved by the Spirit of God, he remained, cultivating some vegetables and palm trees for his own needs and those of the poor in the village, as well as for strangers who passed by. Soon he was baptized in the neighbouring church, and on the same night he received a vision of his future destiny. In an epidemic he devoted himself to the care of the sick; and when he found it impossible to live in solitude because of the crowds that surrounded him, he determined to adopt an anchoretic life. Leaving his dwelling, vegetables and palm trees in the care of an old monk, he went off to seek Palæmon, of whom he had heard.

The Greek account makes no mention of the little temple at Chenoboskion, and although the Bohairic and Arabic accounts do refer to it, they give no support to the theory that Pachomius was a recluse of Serapis, for it was the Spirit of God which moved him; it was to " My Lord Jesus, the Christ " that he dedicated his intention; his return to the temple after baptism would have been impossible had he been a devotee of Serapis; and his work of tending the sick in their homes was entirely contrary to the habits of these recluses.

Further, it is clear that the temple at Chenoboskion had long been deserted and that no recluses of Serapis lived there, for the following reasons: these recluses were found in frequented places, whereas Pachomius went to Schenesit because so few people lived there; he

[1] *Annales du Musée Guimet*, xvii. 6 ff., 342 ff.

was probably alone at the temple, for on leaving he found it necessary to get an old monk to look after his dwelling; the Bohairic account states that it was so called "by the ancients," and certainly implies that it was only known through tradition as a temple of Serapis.

4. *Jewish.*

The Sons of the Prophets were called "the monks of the Old Testament" by Jerome;[1] but they do not appear to have been even ascetics at all.[2] Moreover, their age was very remote: they rose into prominence in the time of Samuel, frequent reference was made to them in the age of Elijah and Elisha, and later their existence was mentioned by Amos (vii. 14), but they disappeared long before the Christian era.

Nor, again, can any connection be shown between the Nazarites or Rechabites and the Christian monks.[3]

But the Essenes and Therapeutæ deserve consideration, because W. M. F. Petrie[4] traces the origin of Christian monasticism to Indian Buddhism through these two communities.

It is a matter of doubt whether all the ascetic practices of the Essenes were really ascetic, or only survivals of primitive habits. Moreover, although they were mostly celibates, some regarded marriage as necessary for the preservation of the race, and were themselves married. Their love of lustrations and ceremonial purity formed a great contrast to the habits of Christian monks. They were divided into four grades, but so great was the distinction between them that

---

[1] *Ep.* 125 [2] cf 2 Kings iv. 1.
[3] See *E R E*, viii p 782.
[4] *Personal Religion in Egypt*, pp. 62 ff.

Non-Christian Ascetic Systems

those in the superior grade were defiled by contact with those in the lower! Further, the great reverence for the Mosaic law, the worship of the sun, the practice of magical arts, and the denial of the resurrection of the body indicated the wide gulf which separated their beliefs from those of the monks. Moreover, the community was probably broken up after the overthrow of Jerusalem in 70 A.D.; Christian literature of the first two centuries does not mention even the name or existence of the Essenes, and it is quite impossible to find any connection between this obscure sect of the first and Christian cenobitism of the fourth century.

It is assumed here that F. C. Conybeare and P. Wendland have disposed of the theory of Lucius that the Therapeutæ were Christian monks of the third century, and that the general post-Reformation view is correct that the Therapeutæ were Jewish ascetics of Egypt in the time of Philo But they cannot be identified with the Essenes, as W. M. F. Petrie claims, for there were many points of contrast between them. Unlike the latter, the Therapeutæ were interested in philosophy, were not engaged in manual work, lived separately from each other during the week, were much more ascetic, and consisted of both men and women. On the other hand, the Essenes surrendered their property for the common benefit instead of to their relations, were divided into grades, and were confined to Syria and Palestine.

Finally, not only were these ascetic contemplatives of Hellenistic Judaism separated from the Christian monks in time by more than two centuries, but their strongly marked Jewish features, their inclusion of women, their interest in philosophy, and the absence of manual work manifest the wide difference in creed and conduct between them and the Christian monks of the fourth century. Moreover, had there been any connection between the two, we should expect cenobitic monasticism to have appeared first, and to have arisen in Lower Egypt.

II

THE ORIGIN OF CHRISTIAN MONASTICISM IN EGYPT

THE origin of Christian monasticism cannot be discovered in the imitation of a non-Christian system, and it is generally agreed that it is to be found in a development of the asceticism which for long had grown up in the Christian church; but no mere account of the general spread of Christian asceticism, even in the East, would seem to be adequate as an explanation of the rise of monasticism in Egypt. It is therefore necessary, notwithstanding our ignorance of the beginnings of Christianity in Egypt, to trace the growth of the ascetic habit there. That can most easily be done in the case of Alexandria; and it will then remain to account for the spread of asceticism from Alexandria to the Copts. When a powerful ascetic tendency has been traced throughout Egypt, an important part of the problem will be solved. But even that alone would not explain the rise of monasticism. It will be necessary to trace the growth of mystical tendencies, and also to discover whether any connection can be established with the Egyptian interest in the future life, whether the circumstances of the Egyptian church were a contributing factor, what were the conditions of Egypt which made it natural that monastic enterprises should be attempted, and what influences were at work which turned men's minds to an ascetic life in the desert, in contrast to the old custom of living an ascetic life in the world. For history points to the general conclusion that the occasion of any popular movement, resulting in a great wave of enthusiasm within the limits of a single generation, is usually found in a combination of diverse elements.

1. ASCETICISM IN EGYPT

A. *Non-Christian*

Asiatic.—The various Asiatic cults were widespread in the Empire, and would be found in cosmopolitan Alexandria, as in Rome. That involved an increase of ascetic thought and practice, for the cult of Ceres had its fastings, and that of the Magna Mater its self-mutilations, the worship of the goddess Mâ from Cappadocia, in addition to self-mutilation, possessed in its priests a kind of mendicant monasticism, the Sun god from Syria demanded asceticism, while the Mithraic cult, with its emphasis on discipline, exercised a wide and deep influence upon the world, and penetrated Egypt as far as Memphis.[1]

Greek.—But in the Roman Empire during the early centuries of Christianity the chief importance and influence of asceticism resulted from Greek philosophy.[2] It came from different schools of thought; Orphism, the later Stoicism, neo-Cynicism, each in its own way contributed to the ascetic thought and practice of the period. Throughout the Græco-Roman world there was a general tendency for religion and morality to be more closely connected in the life of the individual;

[1] F Cumont, *The Mysteries of Mithra*, p. 33.
[2] *E R.E.*, ii. pp 108 f.

Asceticism in Egypt

union with the Divine demanded purity of soul, which was sought by asceticism; widespread was the dualistic view of man, and the conception of the body as the grave or prison-house of the soul.

The Greek population of Egypt was not likely to be exempt from this powerful influence. Indeed, Alexandria, the great centre of Greek culture, was specially associated with two movements that were marked by a strict asceticism.

Neo-Pythagoreanism represented a revival of the doctrines of Pythagoras. It was eclectic in character, but various ascetic features of the Pythagorean system were reproduced. Thus its followers were vegetarians, abstained from wine, depreciated marriage, and laid great stress upon silence. The romantic biography, written by Philostratus (c. 220 A.D.), portrayed Apollonius of Tyana as a perfect model of the Pythagorean life. The latter belonged to the first century A.D., and at sixteen became a devout Pythagorean, spending five years, from the age of twenty-one to twenty-six, under the discipline of silence. He is represented as teaching at Alexandria, where he left followers, and also as visiting Upper Egypt. From an early age he went bare-foot, let his hair grow, was a strict vegetarian, and avoided the use of wine.

The later ascetic movement of Greek thought was neo-Platonism, which originated at Alexandria. This eclectic system, to which reference has already been made, claimed Ammonius Saccas (died c. 245) as its founder. Little, however, is known of him, but he is said to have been formerly a Christian, and his fame rests on the fact that he was the teacher of Plotinus, the chief representative of neo-Platonism. Plotinus

(205-270 A.D.) was born, according to tradition, at Lycopolis in Egypt, became a student of philosophy at Alexandria, and remained there for eleven years as a disciple of Ammonius. He " identified matter with evil, and made purification from the contaminations of sense, withdrawal from the world, and liberation of the soul from its enslavement to the body, the fundamental requirements of his ethical teaching."[1] His life was marked by a strict asceticism: he was a vegetarian and very sparing in his amount of sleep.

Neo-Platonism, which was developed by Porphyry (233-300 A.D.), who laid more stress on asceticism, flourished at Alexandria until the fifth century, and exercised a deep and powerful influence upon contemporary thought, both pagan and Christian.

Egyptian.—For several centuries before the Christian era, Greek influence had grown in Egypt. Greeks had settled in the towns and villages; Ptolemais, in Upper Egypt, was a Greek city, there were many Greeks in the Fayum, and from the time of Hadrian's visit to Egypt Greek influence on Egyptian art became marked, which is seen particularly in the coinage,[2] and also in the portraits of deceased persons from the mummy cases in the Fayum.[3] Likewise in course of time the religion of Egypt came increasingly under the influence of Hellenism. The desire to unify the Greek and Egyptian elements in the population of Alexandria led to the foundation of a common cult. The dead sacred Apis bull became Serapis, and in that Hellenised

---

[1] *E.R.E*, v. 496
[2] R S. Poole, *Cat. of Greek Coins in B.M*; *Alex.*, p xxxi.
[3] P. D. Scott-Moncrieff, *Paganism and Christianity in Egypt*, p. 26 f.

Asceticism in Egypt

form Osiris was worshipped by Greeks and Egyptians alike and became the chief cult of Alexandria, and by the second century A.D. there were forty-two Serapeums in Egypt.[1] Moreover, many of the old Egyptian gods became Hellenised; and although those forms might not be recognised in the ancient temples, they became immensely popular with the people, in whose houses small terra-cotta figures of the gods, especially Harpocrates (or Horus), were common during the third century. But there is also some evidence to show that Greek influence had penetrated even to the Egyptian priests, for Manetho, the Egyptian priest, wrote an account of Egypt in Greek, and was consulted by the first Ptolemy about the introduction of the worship of Serapis[2]; and the sacred scribe, Chæremon, an Egyptian, was a Stoic and became the tutor of Nero.[3] The Hellenic tendency was accelerated by the gradual decay of the old Egyptian religion in the second and third centuries, which came to be less and less intelligible, for hieroglyphics, which were used until about the end of the third century, were read and understood by very few. Another factor was the intermarriage of Egyptians and Greeks, for which the evidence of mummy tickets is available, showing that probably more than a quarter of the population of the lower classes had Greek or Italian blood in their veins.[4]

Therefore A. Erman, writing from the point of view of the Egyptologist, is able to say: " In the centuries following the birth of Christ, Greece obtained increasing ascendancy over the native Egyptian ideas, and their

---
[1] *Ælius Aristid.*, VIII. 56.
[2] Joseph, *c. Apion* , I 14, 26-31 ; Plutarch, *de Is. et Osir.*, 28.
[3] Otto, *Priester und Tempel*, II. 216 f.
[4] Hall, Proceedings of Soc of Bibl. Archæology, XXVII., p. 16 f.

religion finally became a complete admixture of Greek and Egyptian elements."[1]

Now, there was little trace of asceticism in the ancient religion of the Egyptians. The character of the Egyptian was naturally gay; he loved pleasure and the good things of the world, which even coloured his ideas about the life after death; and although he was taught to be abstemious in eating and drinking, drunkenness was common at the feasts. But for the mass of the people life was hard, and there was little gaiety in the life of the labourer. The grandeur and terrors of the desert, as well as the strenuous work before and during the inundations of the Nile, seem to have counteracted the effects of a glorious climate, so that gravity and a serious view of life marked the Egyptian character. But the love of pleasure was characteristic of the upper classes, especially in the later times.[2] Ascetic practices were however known, as we learn from the Book of the Dead, for in each of the two rubrics, attached to one of its oldest chapters (64), it is laid down that " this chapter shall be recited by a man who is ceremonially clean and pure, who hath not eaten the flesh of animals or fish, and who hath not had intercourse with women." Chapter 137A bears a like witness, for it states; " and behold, these things shall be performed by a man who is clean and is ceremonially pure, and who hath eaten neither meat nor fish, and who hath not (recently) had intercourse with women."

In Alexandria, asceticism found an entry through Greek thought, for when the worship of Osiris and Isis was reorganised by Ptolemy, with the assistance of

[1] *Handbook of Egyptian Religion*, p. 224.
[2] cp. L. Spencer, *Myths of Ancient Egypt*, p. 50; A. Erman, *Life in Ancient Egypt*, E.T., pp. 13 f., 34.

Manetho, the Egyptian priest, and Timotheus, the Greek, "the ascetic side of the worship too with its fastings and abstinence from the pleasures of sense, that the soul might lose itself in the mystical contemplation of deity, had a fascination for natures that were religiously susceptible."[1] Reference may be made at this point, if W. M. F. Petrie is correct in ascribing it to a date before the Christian era, to the strange medley of Greek and Egyptian thought, known as the Hermetic literature, which was the work of one or more Egyptians, for there is laid down in Poemander[2] the ascetic principle that one must hate one's own body, if one would love oneself. It should, however, be added that this work has been assigned to the period of 313-330 A.D.[3] And there may be mentioned again the existence of those Egyptian sages, whom Apollonius, the Pythagorean, was reported to have found and described as following an ascetic mode of life, in the first century A.D. Plutarch, who from a Græco-Roman point of view had a considerable acquaintance with the religion of Egypt, wrote an account of the cult of Isis and Osiris, as it was in the first century A.D., and said that renunciation of sensual pleasures was necessary for the attainment of the highest spiritual knowledge and commended the abstinence of the native Egyptian priests, who drank water, abstained from the flesh of the sheep and pig, all kinds of fish, garlic, and during the fasts, salt.[4] "As for wine they that serve the god at Heliopolis do not usually carry it into the temple, for the reason that it is not decent to drink when the Lord and King of day is looking on. The others use it indeed, but sparingly, and keep many fasts where

---

[1] See E. A. W. Budge, *The Gods of the Egyptians*, II. 217.
[2] iv. 6.   [3] E.R.E., vi. 628.   [4] de Is. et Osir., 2, 5, 7, 8.

wine is forbidden."[1] Further, Juvenal[2] provides the following picture of the austerities associated with the Isis cult at Rome. The devotee of Isis " will break the ice and plunge in the river in the depth of winter, or dip three times in Tiber at early dawn, and bathe her timid head in its very eddies, and thence emerging will crawl on bleeding knees, naked and shivering over the whole field of the haughty tyrant. If White Io command, she will go to the extremity of Egypt, and bring back water fetched from scorching Meroë to sprinkle on the temple of Isis."

Again, Apuleius[3] depicts the preparation of Lucius for the initiation to the mysteries of Isis, in which he was bidden to abstain from all pleasures of the table, to eat no living thing, and to drink no wine, and on a subsequent occasion with a like object, to abstain from animal food for ten days, a time, however, which he exceeded in his enthusiasm.

It is clear, therefore, that asceticism entered into Egyptian life long before the rise of monasticism, but there is no evidence to show how extensive it was among the people in general. This, however, does not at all imply that Greek philosophy was intelligible to the ordinary Egyptian; that would not be essential to the practice of asceticism; but the foregoing evidence shows that ascetic habits were at the least familiar to the native, and to some extent, adopted by him.

Jewish.—The most important Jewish community outside Palestine was in Egypt; in the early part of the first century A.D. there were a million Jews in Egypt,[4] out of a total population which (apart from

---

[1] op. cit., 6. [2] vi. 522 ff.
[3] *Met.*, xi. 23, 30. [4] Philo, *in Flacc.* 6.

Asceticism in Egypt

the slaves) was estimated at not less than eight millions in Vespasian's time;[1] in Alexandria two out of five divisions of the city were called Jewish;[2] and Jews were to be found in Upper, Middle and Lower Egypt.[3]

It was inevitable that in such a city as Alexandria the Jews should be considerably influenced by Hellenism, that is to say, they " could not maintain an attitude of aloofness from the culture of the world around them." Consequently an atmosphere prevailed there, favourable to asceticism, which appeared not only in the literature, but in the lives of Alexandrian Jews. Little importance can be attached in this connection to the Book of Wisdom, which belonged to the first century B.C., for, although certain passages (iii. 13 f., iv. i., ix. 15) are sometimes quoted, it is doubtful whether they teach ascetic views of the body and marriage.

But the prophet of Alexandrian Judaism was Philo, who may be taken as representing the atmosphere which resulted from the meeting of Judaism and Hellenism. It has been denied that Philo was an ascetic,[4] for he expressed disapproval of such exercises as fasting, abstinence from the bath, and sleeping on the ground,[5] and he dissuaded the young from adopting the life of a recluse; but he would seem to have recommended that men do their work in life, and not before fifty years of age devote themselves to a secluded life of contemplation.[6] There is, indeed, a strong ascetic vein in his writings. At one time he appears to commend renunciation of the world,[7] voluntary poverty and abstinence;[8] elsewhere he says that he himself

---

[1] Mommsen, *Provinces of Roman Empire*, ii. 258.
[2] *In Flacc*, 8. [3] *H D B.*, v. 96.
[4] E.R.E., 1. 311 f. [5] *quod det pot*, 7. [6] *de profugis*, 6.
[7] *de præm. et poen*, 3. [8] *de mut. nom*, 4.

had often left his friends and kinsfolk and country, and had gone into the desert, although the profit to himself had been disappointing.[1] But further, he asserts that the body is evil by nature and plots against the soul, and then proceeds to say : " the philosopher being a lover of what is virtuous cares for that which is alive within him, namely his soul, and disregards his body which is dead, having no other object but to prevent the most excellent portion of him, namely his soul, from being injured by the evil and dead thing which is connected with it."[2] As Dr. Drummond[3] has said, " this view, logically carried out, is the parent of asceticism." Philo's writings are important for the further reason that he bears witness, especially in the *de profugis*,[4] to the existence of ascetic recluses in and around Alexandria, some of whom were young and wealthy Jews of that city. Indeed, the condition of cities in his day with so much to disgust and disturb would naturally lead those who sought the contemplative life to leave them for solitude in more remote places. Consequently, we are not unprepared to find such a community as the Therapeutæ, to which reference has already been made. They are described in the *De Vita Contemplativa* as living in all parts of Egypt, but mainly near Lake Mareotis in separate huts, which only provided simple shelter from heat and cold. They were placed not too far from one another for the sake of fellowship and protection, but at such a distance that the life of solitude was not interrupted. In each dwelling there was a sacred chamber (*semneion* or *monasterion*) where " they performed the mysteries of the religious life." Therein

[1] *leg. alleg.*, 11, 21.   [2] *leg. alleg* , 111 22.
[3] *Philo Judæus*, 1 23.   [4] cf. *vit. Abrah* , 4.

Asceticism in Egypt

they spent the day, taking with them neither food nor drink, but only the Law, Prophecies, hymns, etc., and occupied themselves in contemplation and studying the Old Testament, finding a secret meaning in its words; and as models they had certain ancient writings. They also composed songs and hymns in various metres and melodies. These chambers they left only after sunset for food and sleep; for, until then, they took no refreshment, and indeed often fasted for three or even six days in the week. Twice a day they prayed, in the morning and evening. Their food consisted of bread, salt and hyssop, and their drink was water from a spring. On the seventh day they all assembled together in a building, where the men and women were separated by a wall; each sat in order of seniority, and the elder expounded the Law. For both men and women joined the community, and the latter were known as Therapeutrides, most of whom were aged virgins (2 ff). The Day of Pentecost was a time of special solemnity, when they were arrayed in white garments, and assembled together, sitting on coarse rugs and mats, the men on the right, and the women on the left hand. After prayer, the president (Proëdros) used to give a discourse, which was followed by the singing of hymns. Afterwards, the holy table was brought in, and a common meal of bread, salt, hyssop and water (hot or cold) followed, at which the younger men served, and these voluntary servants were called ephemereutæ. The night was spent in singing hymns, and dancing after the example of Miriam (8 ff). It is said that on embracing this mode of life they distributed their property among their relations, but probably they did not renounce all, because they had to provide for themselves houses and food.

B. Christian

Growth of Christianity

The beginnings of Christianity in Egypt are unknown, but its centre was Alexandria, for until the time of Bishop Demetrius (c. 188–231 A.D.), there were no other bishops in Egypt; and the rest of the churches, apparently governed by presbyters and deacons,[1] were subject to the church of Alexandria. The Didache suggests the possibility that Christianity spread through the work of teachers who went from town to town, staying only a short time in each place; and this is confirmed by the existence of teachers in the third century. A large number of Jews had become Christian during the second century, if the Gospel according to the Hebrews circulated among them. Moreover, Gnostic sects are known to have been widespread in Egypt, and indeed derived some of their ideas from the religion of the ancient Egyptians. Vigorous missionary work throughout the country was carried on by Basilides,[2] Valentinus,[3] and the Marcionites, for Clement thought it necessary to write a treatise against this heresy. The epistle of Ammon (6) referred to the presence of Marcionites in the time of Pachomius, and Epiphanius[4] stated that the followers of Marcion were still to be found in Egypt and the Thebaid. A fine collection of Gnostic gems and amulets in the British Museum (table case N, Fourth Egyptian Room) also bears witness to the Gnostic activities, and literature is represented by the Pistis Sophia, which

[1] Euseb., *H E.*, vii. 24.
[2] Epiph., *Hær.*, xxiv. 1.
[3] Epiph., *Hær.*, xxxi. 7.
[4] *Hær*, xlii. 1.

Asceticism in Egypt

probably circulated in its original Greek during the third century.

The Montanist movement also penetrated into Egypt.[1]

But by the time of Demetrius it may be said in the words of Harnack[2] that the Alexandrian church was " a stately church with a powerful bishop and a school of higher learning attached to it by means of which its influence was to be diffused and its fame borne far and wide." And so numerous were the Christians in 202 A.D. that Eusebius[3] wrote of multitudes who were martyred from Egypt and all Thebais. During the third century the spread of Christianity is shown by the increase of the episcopate (for Demetrius is said to have consecrated only three, but Heraclas, towards the middle of the third century, as many as twenty bishops, according to Eutych. i. 332), by Clement's statement[4] that Christianity had spread to " every nation and village and town," by the evidence of papyri, libelli libellatici (250 A D.) and seals, as well as by the references of Eusebius.[5]

As to when Christianity spread to the Copts we have no information ; archæology does not testify with certainty to the second century. It certainly had done so by 250 A.D., for the Decian martyrs included some with Coptic names.[6] Translations of the Scriptures into Coptic probably existed in the third century, and the rise of monasticism at the beginning of the next century bore witness to the spread of Christianity among the Copts during the same period.

---

[1] Clem., *Strom*, iv. 13 ; Didym, *de Trinit.*, iii. 41.
[2] *M.E.C.*, ii. 159.   [3] *H.E.*, vi 1, 2.   [4] *Strom.*, vi 18.
[5] See Harnack, *M E.C.*, ii. 158 ff. ; *E.R.E.*, iv. 113 ff. ; P. D. Scott-Moncrieff, *Paganism and Christianity in Egypt.*
[6] Euseb., *H.E.*, vi. 41.

It appears, therefore, that Christianity made great advance during the third century among the native inhabitants of Egypt, although there may have been few adherents in the preceding century.

Growth of Christian Asceticism.—The question as to how asceticism grew up and spread in the Egyptian Church generally is a central problem of the rise of monasticism in that country.

1. It has already been shown that the population of Alexandria and Egypt had become impregnated with ascetic tendencies. This was the case with the chief races, Greek, Jewish and (to some extent) Egyptian. In other words, when Christianity was brought to the various races living in Egypt, it came to minds, of the most earnest at any rate, who had been taught to look upon the world and life through ascetic eyes, and to regard asceticism as the highest ideal, and who had become familiar with ascetic practices. (It is not perhaps without significance that an Alexandrian Christian in Justin's time[1] applied for permission, but without success, to go to the length of self-mutilation, as Origen did later.)

2. Consequently it would be natural to find this ascetic tendency in the early Christian literature of Egypt. Indeed the peculiar circumstances of the Egyptian Church would be favourable, for " ecclesiastical custom had attributed an authority to a great number of early Christian writings without strictly defining the nature of this authority or making it equal to that of the Old Testament. Whatever professed to be inspired, or apostolic, or ancient, or edifying was regarded as the work of the Spirit, and therefore was the word of God." And again, " the content

---

[1] See *Apol.* i. 29.

Asceticism in Egypt

of the New Testament Canon, or to speak more correctly, its reception in the church and exact attributes had not yet been finally settled in Alexandria " at the end of the second century.[1] To this circumstance may perhaps be added the further fact that at the same period " the Alexandrian Church neither possessed a baptismal confession similar to that of Rome, nor understood by ' regula fidei ' and synonymous expressions a collection of beliefs fixed in some fashion and derived from the apostles."[2]

Thus the Gospel according to the Egyptians circulated in Clement's time and was not until Origen's day regarded as an heretical writing. One of its few surviving fragments relates a conversation between our Lord and Salome, in which the body is described as " the garment of shame; " the perfect state is that in which sexual distinctions and relations are abolished, and the bearing of children as the bitter plant of bodily passion is to be avoided.[3]

Similar but slighter evidence is borne by the Oxyrhynchus papyri, discovered in 1897 and 1904, which are probably to be ascribed to the early part of the third century ; both series of sayings appear to show Encratite tendencies. In the second Logion, " Jesus said, except ye fast to the world, ye shall in no wise find the kingdom of God."[4] There is another reference to fasting in the fifth of the *New Sayings of Jesus* which, however, is " broken beyond hope of recovery "[5] Further, Clement preserves the following non-canonical saying of our Lord, " Again the Lord says, he that is married let him not cast away (his wife) ; and he that

---

[1] Harnack, *H D*, ii 60.
[2] Harnack, *H D*, ii 33 [3] *Strom.*, iii 9, 13
[4] Grenfell and Hunt, *New Sayings of Jesus*, p 35.
[5] Grenfell and Hunt, op cit, p 18 f

is not married, let him not marry."[1] A tradition may also be mentioned, which was current in Clement's time,[2] that St. Matthew had lived on " seeds and roots and vegetables, without flesh." This evidence is the more significant when it is remembered how little has survived of the sacred literature current in the Church of Egypt at so early a period.

3. The slow development of Church government in the Church of Egypt[3] also would favour the spread of asceticism, since Alexandria was a great centre of asceticism. The influence of the Church of Alexandria must have been very great, not only because of its prestige, but since it was the centre of Church authority and activity ; from it would come many of the teachers as well as clergy, whose influence would be strongly felt in those parts where they laboured ; and it meant that Christianity would tend to come to the people through ascetic channels.

In this connection we may consider here the teaching of the two great Alexandrines, Clement and Origen.

Clement's position in regard to asceticism is slightly complicated. It must be remembered that he lived in a city which loved pleasure and luxury, and that there were two entirely different doctrines, especially as regards marriage, which he felt bound to combat. One came from the followers of Carpocrates, who advocated licentious living, while the Marcionites on the other hand were ascetic to an extreme degree.

Although Clement did not rise to the full Christian conception, he held no low views about the body.[4] If it had been the enemy of the soul, Christ would not have paid so much attention to the healing of men's

[1] *Strom* , III 15. [2] *Pæd* , II. 1.
[3] Harnack, *H.D.*, ii. 71 f. [4] *Strom.*, IV. 3 ff.

Asceticism in Egypt

bodies.[1] But strangely enough he approved Plato's saying that the soul of the philosopher dishonours the body and seeks to be alone by itself, and did not condemn the belief that the body is the prison of the soul.[2] Probably, however, the solution of this contradiction is as follows: when his mind was fixed on heretics who abused the body either by licentiousness or excessive asceticism, he laid stress on a lofty view of man, but underneath was the influence of his Greek training, which he could not wholly escape, and which explains his tendency towards asceticism. As regards fasting, Jerome states[3] that Clement wrote a treatise on the subject; in *Pæd.*, iii. 12 he referred to fasting, and condemned gluttony.[4] In *Pæd.*, ii. 2 he discussed the use of wine, not forbidding it if used in moderation, but pointing out its dangers, and added " I admire those who have adopted an austere life and who are fond of water, the medicine of temperance, and flee as far as possible from wine, shunning it as they would the danger of fire." But he was careful to note that of our Lord " they say, behold a glutton and winebibber . . . let this be held fast by us against them that are called Encratites." He likewise shrank from severe asceticism in the matter of poverty. Wealth can be a stronghold of evil, but it is not necessarily a hindrance to spiritual progress.[5] It can be well used or misused,[6] but it is good for men to be unencumbered as far as possible.[7] He condemned luxury,[8] and was rigorous on the subject of fine clothes and pleasures.[9]

[1] *Strom*, iii 17.
[2] *Strom.*, iii 3.
[3] *De vir. illust*, 38
[4] cf *Pæd*, ii 1.
[5] *Pæd*, ii. 3
[6] *Pæd.*, iii 6.
[7] *Pæd*, iii. 7.
[8] *Pæd.*, ii. 1; iii. 2.
[9] *Pæd.*, ii 1 ff.; iii. 2 f.

A similar moderation was taught by Clement in regard to marriage. It is shown by R. B. Tollinton[1] that possibly he was himself a married man. He urged the need of purity, upheld the necessity of marriage for the preservation of the race, emphasised its sanctity[2] and repudiated those who said that marriage and generation were evil.[3] Of the true Gnostic he remarked: " wherefore also he eats and drinks and marries, not as principal ends of existence, but as necessary. I name marriage even, if the Word prescribe, and as is suitable. For having become perfect, he has the apostles for examples; and one is not really shown to be a man in the choice of a single life; but he surpasses men who, disciplined by marriage, procreation of children and care for the home . . . has been inseparable from God's love, and withstood all temptation arising through children and wife and domestics and possessions. But he that has no family is in a great degree free from temptation."[4] But elsewhere he praised virginity: " such an one is no longer continent, but has reached a state of passionless waiting to put on the divine image."[5]

As a summary of this enquiry it may be said that " in the background of all Clement's moral teaching there is a certain ascetic strain . . . on the whole it is not the predominant influence, and it is certainly not so in the case of marriage; but it is always there. It makes him suspicious of all that belongs to the domain of sense, emotion, desire. It may be traced backwards to Platonism and the distrust of all that was material; forwards to the monastery and Simon

---

[1] *Clement of Alexandria*, 1. 270 ff. [2] *Strom*, 11 23; 111. 12.
[3] *Strom.*, 111. 12, 17. [4] *Strom*, vii. 12.
[5] *Strom.*, iv. 22.

Asceticism in Egypt

Stylites on his pillar."[1] Indeed, the amount of space he devoted and the importance he attached to the subject pointed to the spread and influence of asceticism in his day.

Origen's influence at Alexandria extended for a considerable period. Born c. 185 of Christian, and probably Greek parentage, he became at an early age a pupil of Pantænus and Clement, and was appointed head of the Catechetical School c. 202. He did not finally leave Alexandria until c. 231. He had attended the lectures of Ammonius Saccas and was thus a contemporary and fellow-pupil of Plotinus. So, according to Porphyry, he was " educated as a Greek in Greek literature " ; but " while he lived outwardly like a Christian in this irregular fashion, he was a Greek in his conception of life and of God, mixing Greek ideas with foreign fables. Plato was his constant companion. He had also the works of Numenius, Cronius, Apollophanes, Longinus, Moderatus, Nikomachus, and the most eminent Pythagoreans constantly in his hands. He also used the writings of the Stoic Chæremon and of Cornutus."[2]

Both his teaching and mode of life were extremely ascetic. He held virginity in high regard for Christians, of whom he said : " So far from defiling themselves by licentious indulgence or the gratification of shameless passion, they in many cases, like perfect priests, for whom such pleasures have no charm, keep themselves in act and thought in a state of virgin purity."[3] He commended " the holy God-pleasing sacrifice " of martyrs, virgins and continent,[4] favoured the celibacy of clergy,[5] but added : " God has allowed us to marry,

[1] R. B. Tollinton, op. cit., 1. 280.   [2] Euseb., *H.E*, vi. 19
[3] *c. Cels.*, vii. 48.   [4] *Comment. on Rom.*, xii. 1.
[5] *Hom. vi. in Lev.* 6.

because all are not fit for the higher, that is, the perfectly pure life."[1] Of poverty he wrote: "If we follow the law of Christ, it does not permit us to have possessions of land or houses in cities. Why do I say houses? We are not permitted to have many tunics or much money, for it says, having food and raiment, let us therewith be content."[2] And again, "I, if I renounce all that I have, and take up my cross and follow Christ, bring a whole burnt-offering to the altar of God."[3]

Of Origen's own austerities, Eusebius[4] says, "Through the entire day he endured no small amount of discipline, and for the greater part of the night he gave himself to the study of the Divine Scriptures. He restrained himself as much as possible by a most philosophic life, sometimes by the discipline of fasting, again by limited time for sleep.... He is said ... for a great many years to have abstained from the use of wine and of all other things beyond his necessary food, so that he was in danger of breaking down and destroying his constitution." Mention must also be made of the extreme to which he went by literally carrying out Matthew xix. 12,[5] an act that was contrary to Roman law[6] and to the feeling of the Church, but not unknown.[7] Origen's asceticism included also a life of poverty, concerning which Eusebius[8] says: "That he might not need aid from others, he disposed of whatever valuable books of ancient literature he possessed, being satisfied with receiving from the purchaser four oboli a day (i.e. sufficient only for the barest

---

[1] *c. Cels*, viii 55. [2] *Hom xv. in Lev* 2.
[3] *Hom. ix. in Lev.* 9. [4] *H.E.*, vi. 3 [5] Euseb, *H E*, vi. 8.
[6] Suetonius, *Hist. of Twelve Cæsars, Domitian*, c 7.
[7] Justin, *Apol.*, 1. 29; Origen, *in Mat* xv. 1; *Nic. Can.*, 1.
[8] *H.E.*, vi. 3.

necessities of life). For many years he lived philosophically in this manner, putting away all the incentives of youthful desires ... and in his zeal he never lay upon a bed, but upon the ground. Most of all he thought the words of the Saviour in the Gospel should be observed, in which he exhorts not to have two coats nor to use shoes, nor to occupy oneself with cares for the future. With a zeal beyond his age, he continued in cold and nakedness ; and going to the very extreme of poverty, he greatly astonished those about him. . . . He is said to have walked for a number of years never wearing a shoe."

With the prevailing tendencies to asceticism in the air it is no wonder that Eusebius was able to say that " by giving such evidences of a philosophic life to those who saw him, he aroused many of his pupils to similar zeal." We learn too from Gregory Thaumaturgus of Origen's ascetic influence ; and his mode of life was followed by his pupil Heraclas, who assisted him at the Catechetical School, and afterwards became bishop of Alexandria, concerning whom it is said that he lived " a philosophic and ascetic life,"[1] and by " the younger Origen," Pierius, " who was distinguished for his life of extreme poverty,"[2] and wrote a commentary on 1 Corinthians, in which he said : " Paul openly preaches celibacy."[3] Moreover, according to Epiphanius,[4] Hieracas, one of Origen's disciples, established a community at Leontopolis, of which the members were severely ascetic and abstained from marriage, wine and meat. But its speculative proclivities seem to mark it as a school or sect rather than a monastic society. The influence of Origen

[1] Euseb , *H E.*, vi 3.
[2] Euseb , *H E* , vii 32.
[3] Jer , *ep* , 49.
[4] *Hær* , 67

was clearly an important factor in the spread of asceticism; in the following century many besides Copts became monks, and it is not without significance that Origen's works were found in the cells of the monks.[1]

4. The work of the Gnostics in Egypt has already been mentioned. Their influence on the Church was probably greater there than elsewhere, because the separation of their communities from the Church was not so clearly defined at Alexandria.[2]

Basilides was at the least well disposed towards practical asceticism, for he is said to have imposed a probation of five years' silence upon his followers,[3] which he probably derived from Pythagorean teaching. Upon the subject of marriage he is reported to have said that some men had a natural aversion to the female sex: such men did well not to marry. Others abstained from marriage through worldly considerations or physical defect, others because the cares incident to a married life would distract their attention from their spiritual interests. If, however, a man by abstaining from marriage lived in a state of perpetual conflict with his passions and of apprehension lest he should be overcome by them, and consequently could not keep his thoughts undividedly fixed upon his heavenly hopes, he ought to marry: to such the Apostle's exhortation was addressed—" It is better to marry than to burn."[4]

But of more importance from the ascetic standpoint was the existence and activity of the Marcionites in Egypt. For Marcion taught the most rigid asceticism; he condemned marriage and even demanded

[1] *H.L.*, 11   [2] Harnack, *H D.*, 1. 250; cp. ii. 323 ff.
[3] Euseb., *H.E.*, iv. 7.   [4] *Strom.*, iii. 1.

Asceticism in Egypt

celibacy from the baptized;[1] and he prohibited all animal food except fish.[2]

Further evidence of ascetic Gnosticism is afforded by the Gospel of Philip and the second book of Jeu. The only fragment that has survived of the Gospel of Philip,[3] which circulated among Gnostic Christians in Egypt, according to the Pistis Sophia, in the third century, and possibly at the end of the second century, displays an antipathy to marriage. In like manner the second book of Jeu, of which the Greek original was composed in Egypt in the third century, inculcated asceticism, for only those who have renounced the world and its goods are worthy of receiving the mysteries; and in the account which represents Jesus sending for wine jars from Galilee, the persons from whom they are to be received must be pure and virgins.[4]

In addition to the Gnostic activities, the influence of the Montanist movement, which also reached Egypt, may again be mentioned. This system at the end of the second and beginning of the third century inculcated a stricter standard of Christian life, in protest against the laxity of the Church. It was based on a belief in the speedy return of Christ, which rendered possessions and marriage of little consequence. Montanism therefore demanded certain forms of renunciation from all its members. While the Church had left the regulation of fasting to individual piety, the Montanists made it compulsory; and as the Church had discouraged second marriages, they prohibited them. Thus, although they were not primarily ascetic,

---

[1] Tertull, *adv Marc*, 1 29 [2] Tertull, *adv. Marc*, 1. 14
[3] Epiph, *Hær*, xxvi 13
[4] P. D Scott-Moncrieff, op cit., pp 183 ff.

their influence would make for the increase of ascetic practices and for ascetic views of life.

5. A close relationship was maintained between the churches of different countries by means of letters, travels, councils, etc. This was particularly the case with such a cosmopolitan and important place as Alexandria, and so famous a country as Egypt. Thus the ascetic thought, practice and literature of other lands could not be without its influence upon Christian life there. For asceticism had long been manifested in the life of the Church. During the second century orthodox Christians as a rule kept closely to the teaching of the New Testament. The body was held in high regard, and the world was not renounced. Sober and restrained views were expressed on celibacy by Ignatius,[1] Hermas,[2] Polycarp[3] and Dionysius of Corinth,[4] and on wealth by Hermas,[5] while no austere or extreme views on fasting appeared to prevail. But Eusebius wrote[6] of the disciples of the Apostles: "Very many of the disciples of that time animated by the Divine Word with a more ardent love for philosophy (i.e. asceticism) had already fulfilled the command of the Saviour and divided their goods to the needy. Then starting out upon long journeys, they performed the office of evangelists, being filled with the desire to preach Christ to those who had not yet heard the word of faith."

Asceticism made the most headway in the East, where the Christian spirit of self-denial was influenced and developed by contact not only with the teaching of Greek philosophy, but also with Gnosticism and the

---

[1] *ad Polyc*, 5.
[2] *Vis*, 1 1; but cf. *Sim*, 9.
[3] *ad Phil*, 4.
[4] Euseb, *H E*, iv 23.
[5] *Sim.*, 1.
[6] *H E*, iii 37.

Asceticism in Egypt

pagan cults of Asia. Consequently the practice of celibacy was not infrequent from an early period in the East. So Justin (c. 100–165), a native of Samaria, a great student of Greek thought, who travelled widely in the East, was able to write : " Many, both men and women, who have been Christ's disciples from childhood, remain pure at the age of sixty and seventy years ; and I boast that I could produce such from every race of men."[1] He was likewise supported by Athenagoras, the Christian philosopher of Athens, " nay you would find many among us, both men and women, growing old unmarried in the hope of living in closer communion with God."[2] From another point of view similar witness was given by Galen (c. 130–200), who was born at Pergamos, in Mysia, and eventually returned there after visiting Smyrna, Alexandria, Rome and other places, for he wrote of Christians, " their contempt of death is patent to us all, as is their abstinence from the use of sexual organs by a certain impulse of modesty. For they include men and women who refrain from cohabiting all their lives, and they also number individuals who, in ruling and controlling themselves, and in their keen pursuit of virtue, have attained a pitch not inferior to that of real philosophers."[3] Two examples were given by Eusebius, as so living at the end of the second century, Melito[4] and Narcissus of Jerusalem.[5] In the third century the pseudo-Clementine epistles to virgins eulogised virginity, and gave a number of rules to certain wandering ascetics ; and Methodius of Tyre (died c. 311) sang the praises of virginity in the *Banquet of the Ten Virgins*.

[1] *Apol.*, 1 15. [2] *Apol*, 33. [3] Harnack, *M E C*, i. 213
[4] *H E*, v 24. [5] *H E*, vi 9

From Africa came also similar praise by Tertullian,[1] who, although he defended marriage,[2] and even drew a beautiful picture of the happy marriage,[3] yet regarded virginity as superior to marriage,[4] and spoke of " the pleasure so bitter of children."[5] He was followed by Cyprian, who also eulogised virginity.[6]

At the beginning of the fourth century we have from Eusebius the names of various martyrs in Palestine: Apphianus, a young man of a very wealthy family, who is described as " despising bodily comforts . . . and paying no attention to his daily needs,"[7] Peter " an ascetic " near Eleutheropolis,[8] Ennathas " a woman from Scythopolis, who was adorned with the chaplet of virginity,"[9] and Pamphilus of Cæsarea, " a man who through his entire life was celebrated for every virtue, for renouncing and despising the world, for sharing his possessions with the needy, for contempt of earthly hopes, and for philosophic deportment and exercise."[10]

Finally, there was the asceticism of the Syriac-speaking Church, for the B'nai Q'yama, " Sons of the Covenant," described also as " solitaries," gave themselves up to celibacy, poverty, vigils, fasting;[11] and it would seem that they were the baptised laity, and that unless candidates were prepared to live celibate lives they were not allowed to receive baptism. Consequently the ordinary Christian only became a full church member at a somewhat advanced age, although after the time of Aphraates married persons were

---

[1] *de exhort. cast*, 1.
[2] *adv Marc*, 1 29.
[3] *ad uxor*, 11. 8
[4] *ad uxor*, 1. 3.
[5] *ad uxor*, 1 5
[6] *de hab virg.*, 3.
[7] Eus., *Mart. Pal*, 4.
[8] *Mart Pal*, 10.
[9] *Mart. Pal*, 9
[10] *Mart Pal.*, 11.
[11] Aphraates, *Hom.*, vi., vii.

Asceticism in Egypt

admitted to baptism, and the " Sons of the Covenant " became a kind of monastic order in the Community.[1]

The existence of a widely spread ascetic tendency, particularly in the matter of celibacy, could not be without its effect upon the Church of Alexandria, which was so situated as to be open in a great degree to the influence of the Church in countries that lay around the Mediterranean.

Thus asceticism was at work in Alexandria and other towns of Egypt. The Eastern with his Asiatic cults, the Egyptian worshipper of Osiris, the Hellenistic Jew, and the pagan Greek were all influenced by ascetic tendencies. From the second century Christianity itself was coloured by asceticism—Christian literature with Encratite tendencies was in circulation; the followers of Marcion were severely ascetic; the Montanists in another way made their contribution ; and Origen, whose influence must have been wide and deep, taught and practised an extreme asceticism. Christianity spread from the Alexandrian Church, whence missionaries went forth and could hardly fail to preach a gospel that was coloured with asceticism. This would be the case in a pronounced degree in the third century, i e. the period when Christianity spread greatly from the Greeks to the natives. Moreover, the first Christian writer, who is said to have published his works in Coptic, was Hieracas, the disciple of Origen, and the head of an ascetic community at Leontopolis.[2]

The native Egyptian might generally be unable to appreciate or understand the philosophical speculations of the day. But that would not prevent the

[1] F. C. Burkitt, *Early Eastern Christianity*, pp. 125 ff.; cf. R. H Connolly, *J.T.S.*, vi., 1905, pp. 522 ff.
[2] Epiph., *Hær.*, 67.

more earnest and devout from understanding and practising asceticism. He would, often by his previous religious experience, but still more by the way in which Christianity was presented to him, tend to read the life and teaching of our Lord and the Apostles, and indeed the Old Testament also, through ascetic eyes. He would, for example, lay stress on our Lord's recognition of voluntary celibacy,[1] as Origen had done to an altogether excessive degree. He would read the story of the rich young man, and would extend its precept " if thou wouldst be perfect, go and sell that thou hast " from the one to the many in the most literal manner, as we know such was the case with Anthony[2] and Abbot Serenus,[3] besides Abbot Theonas who said that this " word of the Gospel sounds daily in our ears."[4] It would seem that the precept " be not anxious for the morrow " and the renunciation of relations and possessions[5] could be best carried out in a monastic life ; so thought Anthony,[6] Abbot Theonas[7] and Abbot Abraham.[8] The words " whosoever taketh not up his cross and followeth after Me is not worthy of Me " was even understood literally by " some most earnest monks " . . . who " made themselves wooden crosses and carried them about constantly on their shoulders."[9] Great importance would be attached to the example of our Lord and the preference of St. Paul for the unmarried life : a bidding to extreme austerities would be read into the same Apostle's reference to Christians as having " crucified the flesh with the passions and lusts thereof," and into his injunction to " mortify your members, which are upon the earth,"

---

[1] Matt xix 12. [2] *Vit*, 2. [3] *Coll*, viii. 3.
[4] *Coll.*, xxi 5. [5] Matt xix 29. [6] *Vit.*, 3.
[7] *Coll.*, xxi. 9. [8] *Coll.*, xxiv. 26. [9] *Coll.*, viii. 3.

while Abbot Abraham made use for a similar purpose of the words " I buffet my body and bring it into bondage."[1] St. Luke's idealised account of the brotherhood existing at Jerusalem in Apostolic days would be regarded as a scheme to be literally carried out; so thought, for example, the Abbot Piamun.[2] The psalmist's words, " My knees are weak from fasting," would make a similar appeal,[3] and monastic ideals would be read into the lives of the great figures of the Old Testament.[4] But such interpretation of the Scriptures would not pre-suppose an acquaintance with the current philosophy.

2. Mysticism in Egypt

Mysticism was not characteristic of the religion of the Egyptians in ancient times ; but the importance of divine contemplation was to be seen in the centuries immediately preceding the rise of monasticism It was traceable to Greek influence, with its conception of God as the Absolute Reality and the desire of the soul to rise above circumstances and thoughts, words and deeds, and find union with the Deity. This influence was to be seen in Alexandrian Judaism, for Philo laid stress on contemplation, and the Therapeutæ devoted themselves to meditation.

But it was not without its effect on the native cults. For Plutarch in his work *de Iside et Osiride* said that the real votary of Isis was he who meditates upon the truth which is involved in the symbols and ceremonies connected with the Deity (3) ; and while this is pursued under difficult conditions during life, the soul

---

[1] *Instit.*, v. 18.   [2] *Coll*, xviii. 5.   [3] *Coll*, xx. 8.
[4] *Coll.*, iii. 4, 6 ; xxi. 4 ; *Instit.*, i. 1, 7.

after death migrates to the kingdom of Osiris where "they hang, as it were, upon him, and contemplate without ever being satiated, and long for that beauty which can neither be spoken nor described" (79). Again, Apuleius writing of the Isis cult, as it was in Rome during the latter part of the second century, described the initiate as enjoying "the ineffable delight of dwelling with the image of the goddess," and the worshipper as gazing on the image in silent prayer and adoration.[1] Porphyry also laid great stress on the contemplative lives of the Egyptian priests, who for this purpose devoted themselves to asceticism, quiet and seclusion from the world.[2] Although these descriptions were written from a non-Egyptian point of view, their agreement points to the growth of mystical tendencies in the religion of Egypt.

Further, while the importance attached by Greek thought to the contemplative life was developed and reached its climax during the third century in neo-Platonism, its influence was seen in Clement of Alexandria, who wrote of the contemplation of the Gnostic,[3] and in Origen, who saw in Martha and Mary the types of the practical and contemplative life, and claimed that only by a life of strict asceticism can a man see God, for "we ought to despise things sensible and temporal and visible, and to do our utmost to reach communion with God, and the contemplation of things that are intelligent and invisible, and a blessed life with God and the friends of God."[4]

Thus the practice of divine contemplation had come to pervade Greek thought, Alexandrian Judaism, and to some extent the native cults; and, as in the case

[1] *Met.*, xi. 20-4. [2] *de abstinent.*, iv. 6 ff.
[3] *Strom.*, vii. 3, 7. [4] *c Cels.*, iii. 56; cf vii. 39.

Mysticism in Egypt

of asceticism, when Christianity spread widely among the Egyptians in the third century, it was at the time when great attention was being paid in the Christian Church of Egypt to the more mystical aspect of religion.

The monastic aim was, as the pages of Cassian abundantly testify, the attainment of perfection, for which purity of prayer was essential. It was for this that multitudes fled from the world and its snares and sought refuge in the lonely life of the desert.

Consequently the subject of divine contemplation was considered to no small extent in the Conferences of Cassian.

Moses quoted the example of Martha and Mary as showing that " the chief good consists in meditation, i.e. in divine contemplation ";[1] and he commended the method of admiring the incomprehensible essence of God, the greatness of His creation, His justice, His daily providence, the vastness of His knowledge and His ineffable mercy.[2] Nesteros said that the contemplation of things divine and the knowledge of most sacred thoughts could only come after pursuing with might and main the improvement of morals and purification from faults.[3] But it is in the conference of Abbot Isaac that the highest stages of the contemplative life are reached, " The end of all perfection is that the mind purged from all carnal desires may daily be lifted towards spiritual things until the whole life and all the thoughts of the heart become one continuous prayer."[4] For keeping up this continual recollection of God, he said that the oldest fathers gave the following formula which was to be used on all occasions :

[1] *Coll.*, i. 8. [2] *Coll.*, i. 15.
[3] *Coll.*, xiv. 1 f. [4] *Coll.*, x. 7.

"O God, make speed to save me : O Lord, make haste to help me."¹ But sometimes a more sublime stage of prayer is reached by minds that have made great advance to the state of perfect purity, with the help of the Spirit ; but this is an ardent kind of prayer "which is known and tried by but very few, and which, to speak more truly, is ineffable, which transcends all human thoughts and is distinguished, I will not say by any sound of the voice, but by no movement of the tongue or utterance of words, but which the mind enlightened by the infusion of that heavenly light describes in no human and confined language, but pours forth richly as from a copious fountain in an accumulation of thoughts, and ineffably utters to God, expressing in the shortest possible space of time such great things that the mind when it returns to its usual condition cannot easily utter or relate."² This kind of incorruptible prayer does not come by gazing at any image, "but with the purpose of the mind all on fire is produced through ecstasy of heart by some unaccountable keenness of spirit."³

Several famous monks are described as reaching great heights of contemplation : Anthony rejoiced in the contemplation of divine things,⁴ and was so persistent that often, as he was praying in a transport of mind, he declaimed against the rising of the sun for disturbing him ;⁵ Paphnutius " in his eager desire for continual divine meditation " plunged into wild and inaccessible parts of the desert, and it was believed that " he enjoyed and delighted in the daily society of angels " ;⁶ Isidore was famous for his ecstasy ;⁷ Macarius of Egypt " was said to be in a continual

[1] *Coll.*, x. 10. [2] *Coll*., ix. 15, 25. [3] *Coll.*, x. 11.
[4] *Vit.*, 84. [5] *Coll.*, ix 31. [6] *Coll.*, iii. 1.
[7] *H L.*, 1.

ecstasy and to spend a far longer time with God than with things sublunary ";[1] and Macarius of Alexandria attempted to keep his mind for five days undisturbed on the contemplation of God, giving this commandment to his mind, " Do not descend from heaven : there you have angels, archangels, the powers on high, the God of all ; do not descend below heaven " ; but he was obliged to leave off on the third day.[2] In short, as Gregory Nazianzen[3] said, the cells of the monk were " holy and divine homes of contemplation in Egypt, where, secluding themselves from the world and welcoming the desert, men live to God more than all who exist in the body."

The subject of the contemplative life may now be concluded with the words of Cassian, which indicate its connection not only with asceticism but with the future life : " the mind is fixed on the contemplation of divine things and is the rather entranced with the love of virtue and the delight of things celestial. And so a man will despise all things present as transitory when he has securely fixed his mental gaze on those things which are immovable and eternal, and already contemplates in heart, though still in the flesh, the blessedness of his future life."[4]

3. Egyptian Belief in a Future Life

The future life after death was the great feature of the Egyptian religion. " The constant presence of the dead in the cliffs and desert overlooking the scenes of their lives, or in later times more familiarly kept surrounding the family life in the atrium of the house

---

[1] *H L.*, 17.   [2] *H.L.*, 18.
[3] *Or.*, xxi. 19.   [4] *Instit.*, v. 14.

preserved a sense of continuity with the other world."[1] Happiness in a future life depended on the due performance of the funeral rites, and the greatest importance was attached to the preservation of the body so that the spirits of the dead might pass between the tomb and the kingdom of Osiris. But the ethical view gradually grew up in ancient Egypt, by which future happiness was regarded as depending upon a virtuous life here. Osiris was the judge of human character; and before the dead could be admitted to his kingdom they had to appear at the Judgment of Osiris, when the weighing of the heart took place;[2] and when in later times Osiris became blended with Serapis, the Osirian faith still survived in the shrines of Isis.[3]

But in the third and fourth centuries A D. there was a gradual decay of Egyptian religious beliefs, and Christianity spread rapidly at that time among the native Egyptians, whose beliefs concerning the future life were spiritualised and raised thereby. The effects of this were seen in two directions

(a) Less significance was attached to the care of the body after death. The practice of mummification and other customs which accompanied it gradually died out among Christians by the beginning of the fifth century.[4] The strong opposition of Anthony to mummification was an example of this tendency.[5]

(b) The monastic records show that great stress was laid upon a strict ethical preparation here for the future life. Monasticism was wholly concerned with the preparation for the next world. To the monk death was no evil thing;[6] indeed no man was to be called blessed

[1] *E R E*, v 236
[2] Book of the Dead, ch 125
[3] *E.R E*, v 476 ff.
[4] *E R E*, IV. 454 f
[5] *Vit.*, 90.
[6] *Coll*, vi 6

Belief in Future Life

before death because the issue of the conflict in which he was engaged had always an element of uncertainty.[1] Moreover the full enjoyment of the vision of God could only be won in the future when a man was free from the distractions and cares which were inseparable from life, even in the desert.[2] So the monk "realises daily that he is presently to depart from this world."[3] The state of the dead was a subject of discussion,[4] and the blessedness of the future was the monk's reward.[5] Anthony's mind was concentrated on the mansions in heaven,[6] and when the time drew near for him to die he "spoke joyously as though sailing from a foreign city to his own."[7] Such was the typical attitude of the monk towards death and the future world, but even if all the references to the subject in the monastic records were gathered together, the importance of the future world to the monk would only be revealed in part. For although a blessedness hereafter was his ultimate goal, it was necessary to stick closely to the immediate aim of "purity of heart, without which no one can gain the end."[8] Consequently all the endeavours of the monk, his renunciations and austerities, his prayers and contemplations, his conflicts with evil, and his whole mode of life had as their underlying basis the desire to be worthy of future blessedness.

It is therefore no wonder that the monastic life laid such a strong hold over a people always deeply interested in the life after death, as pointing a new and higher way when the old religious beliefs were collapsing, to joy and happiness in the future.

---

[1] *Coll*, vi 16. [2] *Coll*, xxiii 5.
[3] *Coll.*, xvi 6; cf *Vit Ant*, 19; *H L*, prolog, 3 f
[4] *Vit. Ant.*, 66. [5] *Coll.*, 1. 10; cf 14
[6] *Vit.*, 45 [7] *Vit.*, 89. [8] *Coll*, 1. 4.

4. Circumstances of the Egyptian Church

The work of Christian teachers in Egypt provided an outlet for the enthusiasm and activity of the laity. As it has been said already, they existed in Egypt no doubt from the early days of Christianity. At the end of the second century " there were still many evangelists of the Word who sought earnestly to use their inspired zeal after the examples of the apostles to increase and build up the Divine Word : one of these is Pantænus," etc.[1] And in the third century Origen referred to the existence of an order of teachers in the church in addition to the orders of bishops, priests and deacons ;[2] he also bore the following witness to the important work done by the laity : " Christians do all in their power to spread their faith all over the world. Some of them accordingly have made it their business to wander not only from city to city but from township to township and village to village in order to gain fresh converts for the Lord."[3] In the middle of the century their importance is shown by the fact that when Dionysius went to the district of Arsinoë to deal with the prevalent Chiliasm, he called together " the presbyters and teachers of the brethren in the villages."[4] But the third century marked the development of episcopal authority in Egypt, together with the control of lay teaching. Of the latter tendency Origen's life was a conspicuous illustration, for the conflict between him and Demetrius was " the conflict

[1] Euseb., *H E.*, v 10.
[2] e.g. *c. Cels.*, iii. 55 ff. ; *Hom.* ii. 1, in Numb. ; *Hom.* vi. 6, in Levit.
[3] *c. Cels.*, iii. 9.   [4] Euseb , *H.E.*, vii. 24.

of an independent teacher of the church with the bishop of an individual community."[1] It pointed to the fact that episcopal authority disapproved of the independent work of the lay teacher; indeed, it would seem that the preaching of laymen in the presence of bishops had been abandoned in Egypt even before the time of Demetrius.[2]

Monasticism was a movement of laymen; it provided an outlet for the enthusiasm of the more earnest Christians. It would appear then that at a period when the work of the laity had been curtailed the monastic movement started by laymen and eagerly supported by the laity in general was a reaction from the official attitude that had been adopted to curtail or take away the old privileges of laymen.

Again, the Church had become secularised to a considerable extent before the reign of Constantine, her claims and demands had been lowered and the leaven of worldliness was working its insidious way. Then came her recognition under Constantine at a moment when so many of the strongest Christians had lost their lives in the Diocletian persecution, as was the case with the preceding generation under Decius, and Egypt suffered severely in those persecutions. Thus at a time when the most virile element was considerably reduced, great numbers of nominal Christians entered the Church, lowering further the standard of her life; and the history of the fourth century discloses the number of time-servers in places low and high, and the semi-pagan lives that were led by very many.

This worldliness of the Church would naturally be felt with keen sorrow and disappointment by the more

[1] Harnack, *M.E.C.*, i 360 ff.   [2] Euseb., *H E.*, vi. 19.

earnest; and monasticism represented the desire to return to the lofty ideals of the New Testament,[1] and was a protest against the worldliness of the Church, from which men turned away to live the Christian life in the desert. And when Arianism, amongst whose supporters this worldliness was particularly marked, arose a few years after the birth of monasticism, it was significant that the monks became bitter opponents of the Arians.

Moreover, when the beginning of the fourth century saw the nominal Christianisation of the Empire, which meant too the cessation of martyrdom, an additional reason is seen for the enthusiasm with which the monastic life was embraced, for no longer could men renounce their lives in suffering at the hands of the State. But this new mode of life offered a sphere for renunciation and suffering, and the monks spoke of themselves as engaged in a contest that was unceasing and very arduous. They were above all men, the "athletes" of Christ, and Christ, the President of the Games, equalised the strength of the combatants, for otherwise "none of the saints could possibly be equal to the endurance of the malice of so many and so great foes, or meet their attacks, or even bear their cruelty and savagery."[2] Their life was likened to a boxing match; the monk planted the blows of continence against his body, and struck it down with the boxing-gloves of fasting; in that way the true athlete of Christ gained a victory over the rebellious flesh.[3] So "in the burning deserts and awful caverns of Egypt and Syria, amidst the pains of self-torture, the morti-

---

[1] *Vit. Ant.*, 2 f.; *Instit.*, vii. 17 f.; *Coll.*, xviii. 5, xxi 7 f.; cf. Jer., *Ep.*, 66.
[2] *Coll.*, vii. 20.   [3] *Instit*, v. 18, 19.

Condition of Egypt

fication of natural desires and relentless battles with hellish monsters, the ascetics now sought to win the crown of heavenly glory which their predecessors in the time of persecution had more quickly and easily gained by a bloody death."[1]

5. CONDITION OF EGYPT

The Roman Empire was in a hopeless condition with its oppressive taxation, extremes of luxury and poverty, slavery, civil wars and moral corruption in the towns, as illustrated by the theatre and the baths. It was indeed a troubled period in the history of Egypt.[2] In 215 A.D. the inhabitants of Alexandria had been massacred by Caracalla, and shortly afterwards a battle was fought between the Roman garrison and the citizens of Alexandria over the succession of Heliogobalus. Later in the century the city was left in ruins and its population reduced to a third of its former numbers as the result of setting up a rival Emperor to Gallienus (260–8); a few years afterwards large Palmyrene forces invaded the country, and an Arab tribe, the Blemmyes, dominated Upper Egypt. In 297 A.D. Alexandria was besieged and a great part of the city was destroyed for its recognition of Achilleus as Emperor. The country generally was in a disturbed and lawless state both in the towns and villages. Moreover, the economic conditions grew gradually worse in the course of the third century; the taxation and other burdens became so heavy that " large numbers of the cultivators of the land were driven to

[1] P. Schaff, *Hist. of Christ. Church*: *Nicene and Post-Nicene Christianity*, vol. 1. p 154.
[2] J G. Milne, *Hist of Egypt under Roman Rule*, pp. 67 ff ; cf. Ammianus Marcellinus, xxii. 16, par. 15 ; Euseb , *H.E.*, vii. 21 ff.

leave their homes and live the life of brigands."[1] A further cause of trouble was the persecution of the Christian population under Decius, Valerian, Diocletian, Galerius and Maximin.

The lawlessness prevailing in the country continued during the fourth century, of which evidence is supplied by the papyri; e.g. in 307 a petitioner from the Great Oasis complained that his wife and children had been forcibly carried off.[2] Robbers were many and fearless.[3] Villages fought one another over fields and water supply.[4] Landing on the shores of the Nile sometimes involved a serious fight with the people of the place, who in one case were described as " desperate characters."[5] Savage races invaded the country.[6] Distress was also caused through the destruction of many towns by inundations[7] as well as through the harshness of the tax gatherer;[8] and in one case failure to pay taxes resulted in the man being scourged and imprisoned for two years, his children sold into slavery, and his wife becoming a wanderer in the desert.[9] The Arian controversy and the storms that centred round the life of Athanasius deeply disturbed the peace of the Church and contributed to the turmoil of the fourth century; the pages of Athanasius are full of references to the outrages of Arians, their ill-treatment of the poor, and the violence of their women.

It is no wonder, therefore, that in such a land men disgusted with those external conditions " turned from the City of Destruction to realise the City of God in the desert and the cell," where they could, in contrast

[1] Milne, op. cit., p. 82.
[2] Grenfell and Hunt, *Greek Papyri*, II 123
[3] H.M., 8, 34; Soz., H E, VI 29   [4] H M, 8; H.L., 31
[5] H L, 35   [6] Coll, II 6, H M, 1.
[7] Coll., XI 3   [8] Vit. Ant., 44.   [9] H M, 16.

Condition of Egypt

with the luxury, sensuality and disorder of the world live peaceful lives of poverty, chastity and prayer. For although the Egyptian was marked by a love of life and appreciation of the pleasures of the world, a pessimistic strain was also to be found as the result of unhappy and disturbed periods in the history of Egypt.[1] This point is important because asceticism is associated with pessimistic views of life.

Indeed, not only such circumstances as the loss or confiscation of possessions, but the peril of death are stated to have operated in the call to monasticism,[2] for those who took part in the prevailing lawlessness, as well as those who suffered from it, became monks. Thus Moses of the desert of Calamus fled " through fear of death which was hanging over him because of a murder ";[3] one, named Macarius, had unwittingly committed a murder as he played with his comrades when he was about eighteen years old;[4] Moses, a priest of Scete, had been a leader of brigands and a murderer, but he became conscience-stricken as a result of his adventures and was converted to monasticism; and through his energetic action a band of four robbers were taken captive by himself, who also decided to renounce the world, saying to themselves " if he who was so great and powerful in brigandage has feared God, why should we defer our salvation? "[5] Cassian[6] acknowledged that such was not the highest mode of conversion to monasticism, but it depended upon the men themselves, for some who had so turned to the desert had reached a very high standard. Mention may be made also at this point of domestic troubles,

---

[1] *E.R.E.*, v. 476, viii. 24 f.; G. Steindorff, *Religion of the Ancient Egyptians*, p 134 f.
[2] *Coll*, iii. 4 f; *H L*, 15   [3] *Coll.*, iii 5.   [4] *H L*, 15.
[5] *H L*, 19.   [6] *Coll.*, iii 5; cf. *H L*, 15.

the loss of dear ones,[1] or a wife's unfaithfulness,[2] which sometimes led to the adoption of monasticism.

6. TENDENCY IN EGYPT TOWARDS THE DESERT

Already the tendency towards a life of isolation in the desert had begun to be manifested. In early days the example of Elijah, the Baptist, and St. Paul, who had sought the desert, at least for a time, does not appear to have had any influence, although Jerome and Cassian saw in such figures of the Scriptures the fathers of monasticism.[3] But from the days of Christ Christians had been conscious of a certain feeling of isolation from the world,[4] as it was expressed later in the Epistle to Diognetus (vi.), "Christians have their abode in the world, and yet they are not of the world." This attitude was naturally strengthened by the early belief in the Parousia, by the opposition and persecution of the State and by the growing corruption and licence around. It is moreover said[5] that during the reign of Antoninus Pius (138–161) an abbot named Frontonius gathered together seventy disciples and took them to live in the Nitrian desert, where they cultivated the ground and led ascetic lives, and considering the climatic and geographical conditions of Egypt it would not be surprising if other cases had occurred, especially in times of stress and persecution. We know certainly of one in Palestine, for Narcissus, Bishop of Jerusalem (c. 200), "fled from the whole body of the Church and hid himself in desert and

---
[1] *Coll.*, III. 4. [2] *H.L.*, 22.
[3] Jer., *Epp.*, 22, 125 ; Cass., *Coll.*, xviii. 6.
[4] John xv. 19; xvii. 14 ff. ; 1 Peter ii 11
[5] *Acta Sanctorum*, April 14.

Tendency towards Desert 67

secret places and remained there many years."[1] But such cases can hardly have been either frequent or well known, for Tertullian in answering the charge brought against Christians of being useless in the affairs of life said: "We are not Indian Brahmins or Gymnosophists who dwell in woods and exile themselves from ordinary human life."[2]

But as the third century proceeded, the tendency towards the desert became marked and can be seen along two lines:

(i.) It is stated by Dionysius, Bishop of Alexandria, that in the Decian persecution great distress came upon his Church, and he speaks[3] " of the multitude that wandered in the deserts and mountains and perished by hunger and thirst and cold and sickness and robbers and wild beasts ... as an example, Chæremon, who was very old, was bishop of the city called Nilus. He fled with his wife to the Arabian mountain and did not return. And though the brethren searched diligently they could not find either them or their bodies. And many who fled to the same Arabian mountain were carried into slavery by the barbarian Saracens. Some of them were ransomed with difficulty and at a large price, others have not been to the present time." It is therefore clear that large numbers of Christians sought refuge in the deserts of Egypt (c. 250), and there is reason for supposing that some of the more ascetic remained after the persecution was over, according to Eusebius,[4] Jerome[5] and Sozomen.[6] One of them (so the story runs), Paul of Thebes, who had fled at the age of sixteen and made his way to a point which few

---

[1] Euseb., *H E*, vi 9. [2] *Apol*, 42.
[3] Euseb., *H E*, vi 42. [4] *Comment* in Ps. lxxxiii. 4
[5] *Vit Paul.*, 4, 5. [6] *H E*, 1 12.

68   Christian Monasticism in Egypt

reached later, continued to live in a cave close to the Red Sea by his spring and date palms unknown, until he was visited by Anthony shortly before his death in c. 340. The details of Jerome's *Vita Pauli*, however, cannot be trusted, for the legendary element is clearly marked, and as it was written before his visit to Egypt his information cannot have been obtained directly from Macarius and Amatas.[1] But that is not a sufficient reason for rejecting Paul's historical existence, since Jerome elsewhere refers to him[2] in terms which forbid the theory that the Vita was a mere romance, and Paul is mentioned also by Cassian[3] and Postumian,[4] who is particularly exact in his topographical details.[5]

But there appears to be no reason for assigning to these refugees any immediate share in the foundation of monasticism; yet they no doubt helped to turn men's minds to the desert as at least a refuge from the ills of life.

(ii.) Of more importance, however, was the custom that had grown up by c. 270 of ascetics living in solitude near their villages, at a time when " there were not yet so many cells (monasteria) in Egypt, and no monk at all knew of the distant desert; but all who wished to give heed to themselves practised the discipline in solitude near their own village." An old man had so lived for many years at Heracleopolis, and there were others in the same neighbourhood.[6] In a little dwelling, built by themselves, they could live a life of prayer and contemplation free from the dangers of society and provide for their few wants by the cultivation of a little piece of ground or by weaving

[1] cf. *Vit. Paul.*, 1.
[2] *Ep*, 22; *Chron. Ann.*, 359.
[3] *Coll.*, xviii. 6
[4] *Dial*, i. 17.
[5] C. Butler, i 231 f
[6] *Vit. Ant*, 3 f.

mats for sale. But this mode of life was not enough for the more aspiring spirits; and as we see in the case of Anthony, who began in this way, and Chronius, who went fifteen thousand paces in the desert from his village,[1] the tendency was gradually to live further away from the villages and the consequent distraction of visitors.

Moreover, one feature of Egypt which no doubt explained in part the rise of monasticism in that country was its climate. There is no country in the world which would be more suitable in that respect for monastic enterprise, as the climate of Egypt is more uniform than elsewhere. Apart from the Delta, which is damper, the atmosphere is very dry and clear, and the dryness counteracts the sudden and great changes in the temperature. It is true that the monk must have often found the winter nights in the desert piercingly cold; even the sternly ascetic Palæmon had a fire at night,[2] but the very small rainfall and the entire absence of snow enabled them to live in such a manner that would have been almost intolerable elsewhere. Together with the climatic advantages, the desert was always a ready and convenient refuge from the world. It offered a vast freedom, and its solitudes were conducive to divine contemplation, and in this respect at least the monks, like many other people, seem to have felt the powerful but somewhat indefinable fascination of the desert.[3]

7. EXAMPLE OF S. ANTHONY

It has now been shown that asceticism and mystical tendencies were very prevalent in the Church of Egypt, that the Copts with their intense interest in

[1] *H.L.*, 47.   [2] *Vit. Pach.*, 5.   [3] *Coll.*, xix. 5

the future life were desirous of inward purity in this world as a preparation for the next, that the more earnest laymen desired to follow closely in the steps of Jesus Christ in a worldly age, that Alexandria and the rest of Egypt were in a very troubled condition from various causes, and that there was a growing tendency towards the desert, in a country which was possessed of a wonderfully equable climate ; this may be said to form the fuel of the monastic movement.

The match was supplied by the example and influence of the great St. Anthony, who can, consequently, be called the founder of Christian monasticism.[1]

Anthony was born (c. 250) in the nome of Heracleopolis in Middle Egypt, at Coma,[2] unless the name be merely a misunderstanding arising from the Greek word for a village, and his parents were well-to-do Egyptian Christians of good family. The *Vita Antonii* (1) depicts him in childhood as obedient and respectful to his parents, attending the Lord's House with them, and simple in his youthful needs ; but although he was not idle, he disliked " letters," and shunned companions of his own age. But about 270 this uneventful life was broken by the death of his father, when he was left alone at the age of eighteen or twenty with one little sister. A few months afterwards he heard the Divine call; one day, on the way to the church, his mind was occupied with the example of the Apostles who had left all for Christ's sake, and when he heard the Gospel read in the service, he took as a special message to himself the words of the Lord to

---

[1] The scepticism as to Anthony's historical existence, associated with the names of Weingarten, Farrar and Gwatkin, has now been abandoned. See C. Butler, ii. p x ; cf i 215 ff., where the evidence is given in full.

[2] Soz., *H.E.*, 1. 13.

Example of S. Anthony

the rich young man.[1] He was not disobedient to the call, but proceeded to distribute his three hundred acres of good land among the villagers and to sell his other possessions, the proceeds of which he distributed among the poor.[2] At first he retained a little for his sister, but when he heard in the Gospel the Lord's command not to be " anxious for the morrow," he gave that also away. So entrusting his sister to a community of virgins (and she later in life became herself " the leader of other virgins "),[3] he started his notable career, and began to lead the ascetic life at first near his old home, but later went outside the village and afterwards to a greater distance.[4] Visiting the hermits of whom he heard, he learnt from all and set himself to imitate their respective virtues. " He observed the graciousness of one ; the unceasing prayer of another ; he took knowledge of another's freedom from anger, and another's lovingkindness ; he gave heed to one as he watched, to another as he studied ; one he admired for his endurance, another for his fasting and sleeping on the ground ; the meekness of one and the long-suffering of another he watched with care, while he took note of the piety towards Christ and the mutual love which animated all."[5] In this way he outstripped all others of his age, but yet so tender was he of the feelings of others that he became greatly beloved. Nevertheless, he found, like all others, that a life of solitude was by no means free from temptation. Thoughts of his sister and the power of wealth tempted him to turn back, evil passions assailed him by day and night ; but he overcame them by constant prayer and greater severity of life. He used to support him-

[1] Matt. xix 21 [2] *Vit*, 2 [3] *Vit.*, 54.
[4] *Vit*, 3, 8. [5] *Vit*, 4

self by the labour of his hands, and all that he did not require he gave to the poor. His food was of the simplest—bread and salt and water; and those humble repasts were not taken until after sunset, and frequently he passed two or even four days without any food. Sleep was reduced to a minimum; often he spent whole nights awake, and when he did sleep, he usually chose the bare ground instead of his rush mat.[1] Such was his mode of life for some fifteen years.

But about the year 285 he crossed the Nile, and found at Pispir a deserted fort, where he made his abode and built up the entrance; and living on bread that was brought every six months and having water within, he remained for twenty years in more complete isolation, never emerging and seldom seen by visitors, devoting himself to communion with God and wrestling with the demons that occupy such a prominent place in the *Vita Antonii*.[2]

This way of living came to an abrupt end (in c. 305), when many, who desired to be his disciples, came and forced open his door. The historic moment when Anthony, filled with the Spirit of God, came forth from his long solitude to guide, advise, and fill with enthusiasm his followers, whom he "directed as a father," marked the beginning of Christian monasticism.[3] But he did not remain long with them; desiring solitude and fearing pride, he joined a caravan, and after journeying for several days in the direction of the Red Sea he came to the foot of a mountain, where there were a spring and a few palm trees. There, in the "Inner Mountain" as distinguished from his former abode in the "Outer Mountain," he found the peace he desired and settled in that place for the remainder of his life,

---

[1] *Vit.*, 3, 5–7.   [2] *Vit*, 12, 13.   [3] *Vit.*, 14, 15.

Example of S. Anthony

devoting himself to prayer and discipline, the cultivation of a little piece of ground and the weaving of baskets.[1]

This quiet uneventful life was broken at times by visits to his disciples at Pispir,[2] and by a journey to Alexandria. He had previously been there in 311 at the time of Maximin's persecution, when he fearlessly strengthened and ministered to the confessors.[3] Again, in 338, at nearly ninety years of age, he was seen in Alexandria, whither his anger against the Arians had brought him to support his friend Athanasius.[4] Among those who visited him were some who came simply for the sake of seeing him, while others sought his prayers, sympathy and healing, of whom mention is made of Fronto, an officer of the Court, and a maiden of Busiris Tripolitana, who were cured by his prayers.[5] Indeed, he was often able to obtain justice and relief for those in distress through his influence with civil and military officials;[6] and so great was his fame that the Emperor Constantine and his sons Constantius and Constans wrote " to him, as to a father, and begged an answer from him."[7]

For the last fifteen years of his life the old man was attended by two disciples, and in 356 he died at the age of one hundred and five years, after bequeathing his two sheepskins to Athanasius and Serapion, Bishop of Thmuis, to the former of whom, the donor, he gave back also the garment on which he lay. According to his express commands, he was buried by his two faithful attendants in a place unknown to others.[8]

The picture which the *Vita Antonii*[9] presents of its

---

[1] *Vit.*, 49 ff
[2] *Vit*, 89.
[3] *Vit*, 46.
[4] *Vit.*, 69-71.
[5] *Vit.*, 55 ff.
[6] *Vit*, 84 ff.
[7] *Vit.*, 81.
[8] *Vit.*, 91-2
[9] 3, 44, 56, 67, 69, 73, 93.

subject is that of a man unlearned, but endowed with a vigorous mind and a remarkable memory which afterwards "served him for books"; physically strong, cheerful, sympathetic, humble, and tolerant, he possessed such personal attraction that a stranger would discover him at a glance in a crowd, although "neither in height nor breadth was he conspicuous above others, but in the serenity of his manner and the purity of his soul."[1] Moreover "his manners were not rough as though he had been reared in the mountain and there grown old, but graceful and polite, and his speech was seasoned with the divine salt."[2] Others were more learned or possessed greater gifts of organisation than he, but Anthony's figure stands above all the rest in the judgment of his contemporaries and of later ages; as C. Butler[3] remarks, "Turn where we will in the monastic literature that had its roots in Egypt between the years 370 and 400, the lofty figure of Anthony rises up in the background of the history. Whether in works which may claim to be history, or in the vaguer traditions enshrined in the Apophthegmata, or in the pure romances, a firmly set tradition ever looks back to Anthony as the inspirer, nay even the creator, of that monastic system, which ... had by the year 370 attained to vast proportions in Egypt and elsewhere." This enormous influence which he wielded was due, not so much to the work he accomplished, but rather to his own character; and his greatness lies in what he was, a man who "concealed under his sheepskin a childlike humility, an amiable simplicity, a rare energy of will, and a glowing love to God, which maintained itself for almost ninety years in the absence of all the comforts and pleasures of

[1] *Vit.*, 67.   [2] *Vit.*, 73   [3] 1. p 225 f

natural life, and triumphed over all the temptations of the flesh. By piety alone, without the help of education or learning, he became one of the most remarkable and influential men in the history of the ancient church."[1]

[1] P. Schaff, *Hist of Christ. Church*: *Nicene and Post-Nicene Christianity*, vol 1. p 188.

III

TYPES OF EGYPTIAN MONASTICISM

THE eremitical life provided the opportunity of complete withdrawal from human intercourse and of uninterrupted contemplation and ecstasy. But it was open to the serious disadvantage that the mind was constantly occupied with the provision of food and work, for in that mode of life the monk could not divest himself entirely of material possessions. Further, he was in danger from vainglory and conceit through the praise of visitors, and was very liable to fall into habits of self-indulgence.[1] The intense individualism of the life involved serious spiritual danger in the case of the younger monks; there was that loss to character which often accompanies a life of isolation, when there is no opportunity of mingling with diverse temperaments and experiences, faults are uncorrected and there are no restraints on the will.[2] Again, the country was in a disturbed and unsettled condition, and the lonely monk was in danger from the lawless.

Therefore experience showed that such a life was, as Cassian saw,[3] best suited for the most advanced in monasticism, and that a common life ("the infant school") was more adapted to the ordinary man who wished to enter upon a monastic career, for a common

[1] *Coll.*, xix. 5, 6, 9; xxiv. 4.   [2] *Coll.*, xviii. 8.
[3] *Coll*, xix. 2.

strength would accrue from a common union, in which the experience and the power of the more advanced would assist the weak.

Consequently Egyptian monasticism in the fourth century showed a strong tendency to pass from the strictly eremitical life to a common life. There was, firstly, the eremite, who lived his hard laborious life away from other monks; this type was not confined to any particular district. Secondly, there was a loose voluntary system, by which men lived to a considerable extent, each his own life, in a large collection of cells. Thirdly, in Southern Egypt there grew up quickly the cenobitic system of a strict common life, founded by Pachomius; and similar communities were to be found in the North during the latter part of the century.

1. EREMITICAL MONASTICISM

This mode of life was that adopted by Anthony himself. Although it may be said to represent the first stage in the evolution of monasticism, the solitary life continued to attract many in Egypt throughout the century. One of the most illustrious was the famous John of Lycopolis, who possessed the gift of prophecy and for thirty years lived in three cells on a lofty mountain, receiving his food of dried fruit or vegetables through a window.[1] Another great solitary was Elijah, who lived for seventy years in the desolate and sterile desert of Antinoë[2]; and in the same region were Solomon, who had lived for fifty years in a cave, Diocles the learned, Kapiton formerly

---

[1] *H L.*, 35; *H M.*, 1; *Instit*, iv. 23–6; *Coll*, 1. 21; xxiv. 26.
[2] *H.M.*, 7.

a thief, and Dorotheus the priest, who ministered to these solitaries.[1] There were also John, who could not easily be found because he was constantly moving from place to place, won great fame by standing for three years, and directed his disciples by letters,[2] as well as the aged Chæremon, Nesteros, and the accomplished Joseph, near Panephysis,[3] whose discourses are preserved by Cassian. The Porphyrian desert (or desert of Calamus), which lay seven or eight days' journey from human habitation,[4] was inhabited by Archebius (afterwards Bishop of Panephysis),[5] Moses who had committed murder in his youth,[6] Paul,[7] and Piteroum who visited a Tabennesiot convent of nuns in search of a woman more excellent than himself.[8] Lastly, Macarius, the younger, who had unwittingly committed murder in his youth, took to the desert, living for three years without a roof over his head.[9] How lonely and terrible was the life that a man could so live was described by Posidonius, when he lived in the Porphyrian district: " The whole year I met no man, heard no talk, touched no bread. I merely subsisted on a few dates and any wild herbs I found."[10]

2. Associations of Eremites

This type of monasticism was founded by Anthony. Drawn together by the hunger for human companionship, the difficulties and the dangers of a solitary life, these monks lived in clusters of cells, and were to some extent under the influence of a superior to whom they voluntarily attached themselves.

[1] *H.L.*, 58. [2] *H.M*, 15. [3] *Coll.*, xi 3.
[4] *Instit*, x. 24; *Coll*, xxiv. 4. [5] *Coll*, xi 2.
[6] *Coll.*, iii. 5; vii. 26. [7] *Instit*, x 24; *Coll*. vii 26.
[8] *H L*, 36 [9] *H L*, 15 [10] *H.L*, 36

i. *Pispir*

The original centre was at Pispir,[1] at the Outer Mountain of St. Anthony, where the fame of his example collected together large numbers who wished to imitate his life. Concerning them the *Vita Antonii* (15) briefly states, " by frequent conversation he increased the eagerness of those already monks, stirred up in most of the rest the love of the discipline, and speedily by the attraction of his words cells multiplied, and he directed them all as a father " ; and their picture is painted in the following words (44) " Their cells were in the mountains, like tabernacles, filled with holy bands of men who sang psalms, loved reading, fasted, prayed, rejoiced in the hope of things to come, laboured in almsgiving, and preserved love and harmony one with another. And truly it was possible, as it were, to behold a land set by itself, filled with piety and justice. For them there was neither the evildoer, nor the injured, nor the reproaches of the tax-gatherer, but instead a multitude of ascetics ; and the one purpose of them all was to aim at virtue." Leaving the solitude of the Inner Mountain, Anthony used to pay them periodical visits, every five, ten or twenty days, to give help and advice.[2] Among the many that so colonized the desert, and owned his leadership, were Hilarion, the founder of monasticism in Palestine (c 310) ;[3] Macarius, the Egyptian, who (c. 330) initiated the settlement in Scete ;[4] Paul the Simple, who left his wife and children because of her unfaithfulness, and lived in a cell some three or four

---

[1] *Vit Ant*, 12, *H L*, 21
[2] *H L.*, 21 ; *Vit Ant.*, 89.
[3] *Vit Hil*, 3
[4] *H L*, 17, *H M*, 28.

miles from Anthony;[1] Macarius of Pispir, and Amatas, who buried their master,[2] Ammonas, Anthony's successor at Pispir, and Pityrion, the successor of Ammonas.[3]

ii. *Chenoboskion* (*Schenesit*)

Near Chenoboskion, at no great distance from Tabennesis, a monk, named Palæmon, was at an early date in the fourth century the head of some ascetics, who lived near him, shared his mode of life, came to him for advice, and cared for him in illness. He is described as a man of few words, who lived a very ascetic life; his meals consisted of bread and salt; and he sometimes devoted himself to prayer and meditation during the whole night. He occupied himself in manual work, the proceeds of which provided him with his few wants and enabled him to give to the poor. The fame of Palæmon is due to the fact that the great Pachomius was his disciple, until the latter departed to found the monastery of Tabennesis. Later, Palæmon suffered severely from the effects of his austerities, and his death was caused by his severe fasting. The close friendship between Palæmon and Pachomius was maintained to the end; and when the old man passed away, he was buried by his beloved disciple.[4] Likewise, there were other associations of ascetics at Chenoboskion under the leadership of Eponymus, at Monchosis,[5] and at Thebeu.[6]

[1] *H.L.*, 22; *H.M.*, 31.
[2] *H.L.*, 21; cf. *Vit. Ant.*, 91, 92.   [3] *H.M*, 17.
[4] *Vit. Pach.*, 3-8.   [5] *Vit. Pach.*, 35.   [6] *Vit Pach.*, 50.

iii. Nitria

But the largest and most famous settlements of monks were in the deserts of Nitria and Scete; they were those which attracted many travellers, and consequently we have a greater knowledge of Antonian monasticism there than elsewhere. The dreary valley of Nitria lay sixty miles south of Alexandria, and extended for thirty miles from east to west and for six miles from north to south between two ranges of mountains, of which one was Mount Nitria. Three distinct monastic districts in this neighbourhood, Nitria, Scete and Cellia, are mentioned by Palladius,[1] Cassian,[2] the *Historia Monachorum*,[3] and Sozomen.[4] But considerable difference of opinion exists as to the relation of Nitria and Scete. The ordinary view regards Nitria as the northern and Scete as the southern part of the valley. But, as C. Butler[5] has shown, this would make the distance between them only ten miles, whereas the above-mentioned writers represent the two districts as separated by a long and dangerous journey[6] in which travellers could lose their way and perish of thirst.[7] It is therefore very probable that Scete lay N. or N.W. of the Nitrian Valley, to the west of the Delta, and that the monastic colony was situated in the heart of the Scetic Desert, while the part known as Cellia[8] was about five miles north of Nitria.

The Nitrian monasticism was founded by Amoun, of a rich and well-born family,[9] whose parents died

---

[1] *H L.*, 18   [2] *Coll*, vi. 1.   [3] 23, 30.
[4] *H.E*, vi. 30 f.   [5] ii. 188 f.
[6] *H.M.*, 30; *Coll.*, vi. 1; *H L*, 26.
[7] *H L.*, 47.   [8] *Coll*, vi 1.
[9] *Vit. Ant*, 60; *H.L.*, 8; *H.M.*, 29; Soc., *H.E.*, iv. 23.

when he was about twenty-two years of age; and since he could not withstand the importunities of his family to marry he persuaded his wife to lead a life of virginity from the day of their marriage. For eighteen years they lived in this way, meeting in the evening for prayers and food They then decided to live separately, and Amoun went to the inner part of Mount Nitria (c. 320–330), where he remained for twenty-two years until his death, which took place before Anthony passed away. Among the monks of Nitria, who by the end of the fourth century numbered five thousand,[1] were Apollonius, who spent twenty years there;[2] Isidore, afterwards Bishop of Hermopolis Parva;[3] Dioscorus, a priest of Nitria and afterwards a bishop;[4] Or, the silent;[5] Pambo, the generous, who died c. 373;[6] Paul, who lived among five hundred ascetics on Mount Pherme, in the North,[7] and Sarapion, the Great.[8] Palladius[9] has given an interesting and detailed account of the Nitrian monasticism, as he found it at the end of the fourth century. In all probability the system by that time had grown and had reached a more advanced stage of development than in its earlier days. The monks lived, however, under no rule, but each was left very much to follow his own inclinations, and the life was entirely voluntary. In their cells the monks lived and worked and prayed, either alone, or sometimes two or even more together. They sang the evening office separately in each dwelling, and so " about the ninth hour it is possible to stand and hear how the strains of melody rise from each habitation so that one believes that one is high

---

[1] *H L.*, 7, 13.   [2] *H.L.*, 13.   [3] *H.L.*, 46.   [4] *H.L.*, 12.
[5] *H.L.*, 9.   [6] *H.L.*, 10; Soc., *H.E.*, iv. 23.   [7] *H.L.*, 20.
[8] *H.L.*, 7, 46.   [9] *H.L.*, 7.

above the world in Paradise." But on Saturdays and Sundays they assembled together, for Nitria had its large church, to which eight priests were attached, although only the senior one ministered—no one else celebrated, or preached, or gave decisions, but they all just sat quietly by his side.[1] The opportunity of Communion was one result of this mode of life, for some of the solitaries must have spent many years without it. Their work consisted of linen-making, so that all were self-supporting. There were also physicians, confectioners, sellers of wine, as well as seven bakeries. It is told of Apollonius, a Nitrian monk, that since he knew no handicraft and could not write, he used to buy from Alexandria and take round eggs, cakes, raisins, drugs, and other articles needed by the monks and the sick.[2] Great importance was attached to the learning of the Scriptures by heart; Ammonius was celebrated in this respect, and could repeat the whole of the Old and New Testaments.[3] The writings, too, of Origen[4] were found in the cells. The value of work, especially manual labour, was recognised not only for the relieving of want, but also as a great preventive of accidie, particularly among the younger monks; that weariness of heart which the monk knew so well, when at times he was filled with dislike for the place, disgust for his cell, contempt for his brethren, and weariness of his work. So Cassian relates an old saying current in Egypt that " a monk who works is attacked by but one devil: but an idler is tormented by countless spirits."[5] Even strangers, who could remain in the guest-house adjoining the Nitrian Church, for as long as two or

---

[1] *H L.*, 7.   [2] *H.L.*, 13.   [3] *H L.*, 11.
[4] *H.L.*, 11; cf. Sulp., *Dial.*, 1. 6.   [5] *Instit.*, x. 23.

three years, were obliged, after a limited period, to work either in the garden, bakery, kitchen, etc., or in study, if they were sufficiently educated. Their food was very simple, and some were of course more austere in their mode of life than others. A feature of Nitria was that the use of wine was allowed. Some attempt was made to preserve discipline, for near the church there were three palm trees, on each of which hung a whip, one for punishing thieves, another for dealing with strangers, and a third for refractory monks; the culprit was brought to the tree and received the stripes appointed. The writer of *Historia Monachorum* preserves a picture of the reception of his party by the Nitrian monks, who saw the visitors from a long distance and vied with one another in their welcome; some brought water, others washed their feet or their garments, some provided food, others again gave instruction; and the same writer bears witness to the affection of the monks for one another.[1] From time to time communications passed between the Nitrian monks and those of Anthony; Amoun himself was a frequent visitor at Pispir; but the total distance between Nitria and Anthony's dwelling-place was a thirteen days' journey.[2]

iv. *Cellia*

Cellia, or Cells, were the abode of six hundred hermits, who lived in numerous little dwellings, which were placed at such distance that they could neither see nor hear one another.[3] There appears to have been a church in that settlement, for not only do Sozomen[4] and Palladius[5] speak of Macarius as its

[1] *H.M.*, 23.   [2] *Vit. Ant*, 60.   [3] Soz., *H.E.*, vi 31.
[4] *H.E.*, vi. 29.   [5] *H L.*, 18.

priest, but an incident is recorded when the church key was lost, and a communion in church at Epiphany is mentioned.¹ There they assembled on Saturdays and Sundays. But they did not communicate much with one another, except for spiritual profit.²

Macarius, the Alexandrian, was remarkable for the spirit of emulation in his ascetic practices, and for possessing four cells in the different districts, Scete, Libya, Nitria and the Cells, of which some were without windows; one was so narrow that he could not stretch himself, and another was large enough for the reception of visitors. It is stated that he was always cheerful to his visitors, and by the affability of his manners led many young men to asceticism. He visited Tabennesis and astonished Pachomius and his monks by his feats of fasting. He died (*c.* 393) almost a centenarian.³ Evagrius, a Cappadocian, who had fallen in love with a nobleman's wife at Constantinople, and after meeting Melania at Jerusalem, confessed to her his sin, and having spent two years in Nitria, lived for fourteen years in Cellia.⁴ He was the author of various books;⁵ and it is recorded of him that "he wrote beautifully the Oxyrhynchus characters," which denote "some sort of uncial writing distinctive of manuscripts *de luxe.*"⁶ Another resident, Marcus, achieved great fame for his meekness and continency, and was said to have learnt the Old and New Testaments by heart; and Theodore, who discoursed on the death of the saints,⁷ also dwelt in the same district.

[1] *H.L.*, 38. [2] Soz., *H E.*, VI. 31.
[3] *H.L.*, 18; *H.M.*, 30; Soc , *H.E* , IV. 23.
[4] *H.L.*, 38. [5] Soc., *H.E.*, IV. 23.
[6] C. H. Turner, *J.T.S.*, 1905, p. 350. [7] *Coll.*, VI.

v. Scete

The colony at the distant and barren Scete, "where are the most excellent monastic fathers, and where all perfection flourishes,"[1] owed its foundation to Anthony's famous disciple Macarius, the Egyptian, or the Great, who was born c. 300, and after leaving Anthony settled in Scete (c. 330), where with two disciples he practised great self-denial. Palladius[2] mentions his curious device to escape visitors; he possessed both a cell and a cave, which he connected by a tunnel of half a mile, and by passing from his cell in this way he was able to obtain the solitude and freedom from distraction that he desired. To Macarius are attributed Homilies, Epistles and many Apophthegmata.

The Scetic monks included Daniel,[3] Isidore[4] and Paphnutius, all of whom were priests, and the last, renowned for patience, had his cell five miles from the church, but did not fail to attend on Saturdays and Sundays;[5] Moses, the Robber, who became a priest, left seventy disciples, and performed amazing austerities in the matter of sleep;[6] Pachon, who was visited by Palladius after he had spent forty years in his cell and had overcome evil thoughts by self-inflicted tortures;[7] Ptolemy, who lived in the more remote and waterless district known as Klimax, and later fell away;[8] Serapion, who discoursed to Cassian on the eight principal faults;[9] and Moses, of Scete, one of the most "splendid flowers" of monasticism, whose

---

[1] Coll., 1. 1.   [2] H L., 17; cf. H.M., 28.   [3] Coll., iv. 1.
[4] H.L., 19.   [5] Coll., iii. 1; xviii 15   [6] H.L., 19.
[7] H.L., 23.   [8] H.L., 27.   [9] Coll., v

views on the aims of the monks are preserved by the same writer.[1]

Only a few scattered references are made to the mode of life at Scete. There were four churches, each with its own priest;[2] the monks attended on Saturdays and Sundays for the Holy Communion,[3] and Abbot John is named as the steward of Scete, and had the management of the church by the appointment of the priest Paphnutius.[4] Life was very hard in this desert, for apart from the severity of self-imposed austerities, water could only be found at a distance varying from half a mile to five miles;[5] and some lived far away, for an old man is mentioned as being eighteen miles from the church, and when a present of figs arrived it was remarked that such had never been seen there before.[6] But although they were so far removed from the world, the monks there learnt that no distance could deliver them from fierce temptation.[7] A high moral standard prevailed, for when a case of supposed stealing occurred it was described as "a new and unheard-of crime, such as no one remembered ever to have been committed in that desert before that time and which has never happened since." But on that occasion common action was taken, for all were kept in church while certain selected brethren searched the cells, and a penance was imposed on the apparent offender.[8] Like other monks, they were engaged in work at which they learnt and repeated by heart the Bible;[9] and one on his way to Scete is described as repeating during the journey the Epistle to the Hebrews, the Book of Isaiah, part of Jeremiah, the

---

[1] *Coll* , 1.   [2] *Coll.*, x 2.   [3] *Coll* , iii. 1 ; xviii. 15.
[4] *Instit* , v. 40   [5] *H L.*, 19, 47.   [6] *Instit.*, v 40.
[7] *H.L.*, 19, 23.   [8] *Coll* , xviii. 15.   [9] *Instit.*, xi. 16.

Gospel of St. Luke and the Proverbs, in addition to other passages.[1] Cassian relates of them that their mats were used for sitting and sleeping, while bundles of papyrus formed a seat at services and a pillow at night.[2] Visitors came to see them (e.g. Cassian), and the monks at times visited one another, and an amusing picture is preserved of eavesdropping, when a monk was heard to be giving in his lonely cell a stirring address, as if he were in church.[3]

vi. *Various Associations, etc.*

Other colonies were established near Alexandria, where Palladius saw as many as two thousand monks,[4] and at Rhinocorura under Dionysius;[5] there were great settlements near Babylon and Memphis;[6] in the neighbourhood of Heracleopolis a few gathered round Paphnutius,[7] and near the village of Phœnice Chronius dwelt with two hundred others;[8] large numbers of monks and nuns congregated at Oxyrhynchus, famous for their deeds of mercy,[9] and near Achoris Apelles the smith exercised his craft for the monks who dwelt there.[10]

A few particulars are given of three other colonies. In the Arsinoite regions there were one thousand monks under the guidance of the priest Serapion, who "taught all to earn their provisions by their labours and to provide for others who were poor. During harvest time they busied themselves in reaping for pay; they set aside sufficient corn for their own use, and shared it with the rest of the monks."[11] Or in the

---

[1] *H L.*, 26.　　[2] *Coll*, 1 23.　　[3] *Instit.*, xi. 16.
[4] *H L.*, 7.　　[5] Soz, *H.E.*, vi. 31.　　[6] *H.M*, 20.
[7] *H M.*, 16　　[8] *H L*, 47.　　[9] *H.M.*, 5.
[10] *H M.*, 14　　[11] Soz, *H.E.*, vi. 28; cf. *H.M.*, 20.

Thebaid was the head of one thousand monks; and a description is given of the rise of a monastic colony, for he and those with him built cells for newcomers, one spreading the mud, others bringing bricks or cutting down wood.[1] There was also an association of one hundred monks in the Thebaid, whose abbot was the priest Dioscorus, and it is said that he laid great stress on their preparation for the Communion.[2]

The food in all these monastic colonies was very simple; they had their one meal of dinner at the sixth or ninth hour,[3] although some famous ascetics fasted until evening. Except on fast days, the monks did not scruple to break their fast on the arrival of visitors.[4] Some went to great lengths in their abstinence; Moses, of Scete, once was in the habit of going without food for several days;[5] some abstained from bread and lived on nothing but beans, or vegetables, or fruits, or herbs; but such extremes were not recommended,[6] nor did the greediness of those who fasted in order to be able to have a large meal command approval.[7] It was usually felt that moderation in fasting should be observed,[8] and the amount of food should vary according to individual age and strength.[9] For some could fast more rigorously than others. "The sickly food of moistened beans does not agree with everybody," nor does a diet of fresh vegetables or dry bread alone; for some two pounds are not enough, for others six ounces are too much.[10] The canonical allowance of bread was fixed at two biscuits, which scarcely weighed a pound,[11] and it was considered

---

[1] *H.M.*, 2.   [2] *H.M.*, 22; Soz., *H.E.*, vi. 28.
[3] *Coll.*, ii. 25 f.; cf. xxi. 11, 23.   [4] *Instit.*, v. 24.
[5] *Coll.*, ii. 17.   [6] *Coll.*, ii. 19; *Instit.*, v. 23.
[7] *Coll.*, ii 24.   [8] *Instit.*, v. 9.   [9] *Coll.*, ii. 22.
[10] *Instit*, v. 5.   [11] *Coll.*, ii. 19, 26.

advisable to keep one of them until the evening in case visitors arrived and courtesy demanded the partaking of food with them.[1] But the Abbot John lamented the habits of self-indulgence which had grown up. Thus in former times the year's allowance of oil was one pint and a modius of lentils for visitors, but in his day two or three times as much were used, for instead of a single drop of oil being mixed with vinegar or sauce, they had much more than was necessary, as well as an Egyptian cheese. But his indignation was great concerning the keeping of a blanket in the cells "under the pretence of hospitality," which he could "not mention without shame."[2] Cassian thus describes a Sunday's "most sumptuous repast," which represented the height of luxury that it was considered wrong to exceed in that desert—a decoction with a liberal amount of oil, table salt, three olives each, a basket of parched vetches called trogalia, of which each had five grains, two prunes and a fig.[3]

They slept only for a short time before dawn.[4] Visits from other monks were to be welcomed, not merely as an opportunity for the practice of patience, but also because refreshment of mind was good for all.[5] Presents were sometimes made from one monk to another, e.g. of grapes and wine.[6] It was a common practice, especially for the younger monks, to confess their faults to wise and experienced brethren and to seek their counsel; such visits were to be received with kindness and sympathy.[7]

---

[1] *Coll.*, ii. 26. [2] *Coll.*, xix 6.
[3] *Coll.*, viii. 1. [4] *Coll.*, vii. 34
[5] *Coll.*, xxiv. 20 [6] *Coll.*, xvii 24.
[7] *Coll.*, ii. 11, 13

3. Cenobitic Monasticism

i. *Community of Aotas*

The first monk who attempted to establish the cenobitic life was Aotas, but it is stated that in the judgment of Anthony he failed because he did not wholeheartedly devote himself to the work. Consequently, as no cenobite community was in existence at the time,[1] the institution of that mode of life is to be attributed to Pachomius.

ii. *Pachomian System*

History. Pachomius was born c. 292 (or 285, according to Grützmacher) of pagan parents in the Upper Thebaid.[2] For a short time, at the age of twenty, he was in the army raised by Constantine. It proved a momentous experience to the young man, for he had the opportunity of seeing the practical charity of the Christians who brought food and drink to the soldiers, with the result that he resolved to become a Christian.[3] He dedicated himself to his newly-found religion as follows : " O God, the Maker of heaven and earth, if Thou wilt deign to regard me unworthy, as I am, that I may know Thee, the only true God, and Thou wilt deliver me from this affliction, I will follow Thy will all the days of my life, and having love towards all men, I will serve them in accordance with Thy command."[4] Constantine's victories enabled Pachomius to obtain a speedy release from the army, whereupon he made his way to the Upper Thebaid and

---

[1] *Vit. Pach.*, 77
[2] Near Latopolis or Esneh, add the Bohairic and Arabic lives, *Annales*, pp 2, 339.   [3] *Vit*, 1–3.   [4] *Vit.*, 3.

came to Chenoboskion (Schenesit). There he received elementary instruction in the Christian faith, and was baptised in the village church. On the night of his baptism a vision came to him which revealed the greatness of his future. It has already been shown that there are no grounds for supposing that Pachomius was a converted monk of Serapis. But about this time it is stated that he was invited to join the Meletians and also the Marcionites.[1] Then hearing of the head of some ascetics, named Palæmon, he went forth to join him. Pachomius, however, lived on more intimate terms with Palæmon than did the others, for he shared his dwelling, ate and worked with him.[2] But on a certain day he went further than usual into the desert to the village of Tabennesis on the eastern bank of the Nile near Tentyra (Denderah), and as he prayed he heard a celestial voice saying, " Remain here and build a monastery, for many men will come to you to become monks."[3] He then, with the assistance of Palæmon, built a cell in that place and left his old master. This was the beginning of the great movement that is associated with his name.

It is difficult to attach dates to these events. But if reliance can be placed upon the Bohairic account,[4] which states that Pachomius remained for three years in Chenoboskion and seven years with Palæmon, it would bring the foundation of Tabennesis, allowing that he was about twenty-one years of age when he left the army, to the year 323 (or 316 if 285 was the date of his birth), which would give sufficient time for the fame of Pachomius to have reached Athanasius before his consecration in 328.[5]

[1] *Ep. Ammon* , 6.   [2] *Vit.*, 4 ff.   [3] *Vit.*, 7.
[4] *Annales*, pp. 10, 25.   [5] *Annales*, p 40.

Pachomian System

We next hear[1] of his older brother John coming to him; but their ideals were different, and the former wished to live as an anchorite. However, three men came to join him whose names were Psentæsis, Surus, and Psois,[2] who were followed by Pecusius, Cornelius, Paul, another Pachomius, John and Theodore.[3] The numbers increased rapidly, and very soon there was a hundred.[4] When the monastery at Tabennesis proved insufficient, another was built two or three miles away at Pabau,[5] or Proou,[6] to the north of Tabennesis on the eastern bank of the Nile. This establishment was ordered on the same lines as the first, and soon grew largely. Not only did individuals come to Pachomius, but associations of ascetics began to join, of which the first dwelt at Chenoboskion, at the head of whom had been Eponymus. There Pachomius ordered the life of this new community and placed some of the monks of Tabennesis and Pabau. This was followed by similar associations at Monchosis or Temouschons,[7] and Thebeu.[8] Further away in the neighbourhood of Panopolis (Akhmim), on the eastern bank of the Nile,[9] two monasteries were built, one at Tase, the other at Tismenæ, to the care of which Petronius was appointed;[10] and by the wish of Arius, Bishop of Panopolis, a third monastery was built near his city, of which Samuel was placed in charge.[11] A ninth monastery was erected at Pachnoum (or Pichnoum) in the neighbourhood of Latopolis, of which Surus was the head, and he was succeeded by Macarius.[12] Meanwhile Pachomius changed his residence from Tabennesis to Pabau, which henceforth

[1] *Vit.*, 9. [2] *Vit.*, 17. [3] *Vit.*, 18. [4] *Vit.*, 18.
[5] *Vit.*, 52. [6] *Vit.*, 35. [7] *Vit.*, 35. [8] *Vit.*, 50.
[9] *Vit.*, 51; *H.L.*, 32. [10] *Vit.*, 52, 74. [11] *Vit.*, 51.
[12] *Vit.*, 52, 78.

became the head monastery of the Pachomian system [1] In 346, soon after Easter, a pestilence broke out in the monasteries and carried off over a hundred of the monks, amongst whom was the founder. Two days before his death, which occurred on May 9th, Pachomius was asked by the brothers to name his successor, and he appointed Petronius, who was the superior of Tismenæ.[2] But he also fell sick and died about two months afterwards.

The successor whom he appointed was Orsisius, the head of Chenoboskion.[3] Under him the communities increased and their prosperity grew. But the new wealth nearly produced a rupture in the monasteries, for Apollonius, the superior of Monchosis, opposed the system by which the revenues were administered by the chief steward of Pabau, and wished to control those of his own monastery. The Superior-General was openly defied, and it seemed as if the work of Pachomius was to be marred by a schism. But happily Orsisius took the step in 350 of appointing Theodore as his coadjutor, and retired to Chenoboskion, leaving the real control to him.[4] It was a fortunate choice, for Theodore ruled the monasteries well and wisely for eighteen years, and restored peace and unity. Theodore had had an interesting history. Born of distinguished Christian parents, he was about to take part one day in some festivities at his home when he suddenly felt their incongruity and refused to be present. After a time he left home and joined an association of ascetics in the nome of Latopolis.[5] But when he heard of Pachomius's new system which had recently been inaugurated, he made his way to

[1] *Vit.*, 50.   [2] *Vit.*, 74.   [3] *Vit.*, 75 f.
[4] *Vit.*, 81-5.   [5] *Vit.*, 23.

Pachomian System

Tabennesis and joined Pachomius when he was about fourteen years old. Theodore became greatly beloved by Pachomius on account of his spiritual progress.[1] When Pachomius moved to Pabau, he placed Tabennesis in the charge of Theodore, who was then about thirty years of age;[2] and it had been his intention,[3] and was the wish of the monks, that Theodore should, after the death of Pachomius, become the Superior-General. However, when Pachomius became ill, Theodore did not sufficiently oppose those expressed wishes of the monks, was consequently deprived of his offices and did not receive the appointment.[4] But notwithstanding these severe measures, Pachomius gave his beloved disciple the charge of burying his body in a secret place.[5] After the accession of Orsisius, Theodore became the head of the bakers at Pachnoum.[6] Then the threatened schism came, and the old disciple of the founder was given the direction of the community. Under his administration two monasteries, Obi and Kaios, were built near Hermopolis Magna (Schmoun), on the western bank of the Nile, and another near Hermothis,[7] while mention is also made of a monastery built by his direction near Ptolemais.[8] On April 27th, 368, the able coadjutor of Orsisius died,[9] and the latter, whom Theodore always recognised as his head by going to him for counsel,[10] and who appears in later years to have resumed some part in the direction of the monasteries,[11] again exercised the full functions of Superior-General.[12]

Little is known of the history of the Pachomian monasteries during the remainder of the fourth

---

[1] *Vit.*, 24–5.   [2] *Vit.*, 50.   [3] *Vit.*, 25.   [4] *Vit.*, 68.
[5] *Vit.*, 75.   [6] *Vit.*, 78.   [7] *Vit.*, 86.   [8] *Ep Amm.*, 17.
[9] *Vit.*, 94.   [10] *Vit.*, 83. [11] *Vit.*, 93. [12] *Vit.*, 95.

century; and there is no record of the length or character of the rule of Orsisius, for the *Doctrina Orsisii* consists of spiritual exhortations to the monks, and especially to those in authority, with many quotations from the Scriptures. But Jerome,[1] in the year 404, adds that a Pachomian monastery existed far away at Canopus, close to Alexandria; and this statement is supported by fragments of a Coptic history of Alexandria, which attributed it to the desire of the patriarch Theophilus, as well as by later evidence.[2]

Development of rules. The organisation of the monasteries was gradually built up according to the increasing needs of the community. Thus the *Vita Pachomii*[3] states that the founder gave various rules to his monks from time to time, which were the result of his thought, prudence and experience, and that he wrote many detailed letters as well to the heads of the monasteries.[4] An account is given in *Vit.* 19[5] of the early stages, when it is shown how Pachomius placed the most suitable monks over the various duties connected with the community, in a way which corresponds with the more developed system described by Jerome. But in the course of time a legend of the supernatural origin of the rules arose, for Palladius[6] said that a tablet of the rules was given to Pachomius by an angel, and Sozomen[7] even adds that it still existed among the monks. There are, however, certain disputed points in the rules, for Palladius[8] states that the monks underwent a three years' probation, were divided into twenty-four sections named

[1] *Reg. Præf.*, 1. [2] Ladeuze, p. 202.
[3] 10, 16, 17, 27, 28, 57, 60, 63. [4] *Vit.*, 63.
[5] cp. 18. [6] *H.L.*, 32; cf. Jerome, *Reg. Præf.*, 9.
[7] *H.E.*, III. 14. [8] *H.L.*, 32.

Pachomian System 97

after the letters of the Greek alphabet, lived three in a cell, had special seats for sleeping, and ate their meals at various hours. He also adds that strange monks were not received in the monastery, unless they were on a journey. But on the other hand there is no reason to distrust the accuracy of Palladius. The following suggestions are offered as a solution of the problem:

(1.) *The three years' probation.* It is true that the *Vita*[1] seems to show that monks were received after a preliminary examination only. But there is no reason why later (for Palladius was in Upper Egypt from 406 to 412) a novitiate should not have grown up, after the original of Jerome's translation had been composed. Its existence is indeed suggested by Cassian,[2] who says that at first they assisted in the guest-house for a year; and if a monk was suitable, his old clothes were given to the poor; otherwise they were returned to him, and he left the monastery[3] Moreover, newcomers, we know, were instructed in the rules, had to learn twenty psalms and two epistles of the New Testament and were required to be able to read[4]

(2.) *The seats for sleeping.* It is clear that Jerome did not know of them,[5] but they also were a later development, for both Palladius and Sozomen[6] refer to them; the latter adds further details, and the *Doctrina Orsisii* (21) mentions a bed.

(3.) *The reception of strange monks.* The large number of monks in the country would naturally demand in course of time stricter rules as to their reception.

(4.) *The twenty-four sections.* According to Palladius

---

[1] 16, 25, 60.   [2] *Instit.*, iv. 7.   [3] *Instit*, iv 6.
[4] *Reg.*, 139.   [5] *Reg.*, 88.   [6] *H.E*, iii. 14.

G

the knowledge of the private meaning attached to each letter was confined to Pachomius, and the senior and most spiritual monks. It seems natural and reasonable to connect this plan with the hidden language, in which Pachomius is described as writing to the superiors of the monasteries.[1] Moreover, "Pachomius might be imagined distinguishing the twenty-four Greek letters of the alphabet by their use as numerals for which purpose he would never have seen the seven Coptic letters employed."[2]

(5.) *The meals at different hours, and three monks to a cell.* Normally, as it will be seen, this does not appear to have been the case. But if a monastery received a sudden and considerable addition of monks, there must have been a time, often prolonged, before the necessary work of enlarging the refectory and the houses could take place. Indeed, at Pabau with its great numbers, especially by the beginning of the fifth century, it might have been a more or less permanent arrangement, through lack of sufficient accommodation to feed thirteen or fourteen hundred at one time and to provide separate cells for so many.

Consequently the chief inaccuracy of Palladius would be his assumption that the customs he saw were part of an original and universal plan, which would be a natural mistake, as he accepted the angelic origin of the rules.

But since Jerome's Latin translation of the rules[3] agrees with what is known of early Pachomianism, it may be taken to represent the development of the original rules and to describe those that existed in the

---

[1] *Vit.*, 63; *Epp. Pach.*
[2] W. E Crum, *Egypt. Explor. Fund, Archæol. Report*, 1898–9, p. 56.
[3] A.D. 404

Pachomian System

latter part of the fourth century, while the account of Palladius no doubt represents the customs he saw at the beginning of the fifth century, which may have grown up some years before 400 A.D.

The Buildings. Each monastery was surrounded by a wall,[1] and in that enclosure were the church,[2] the place of general assembly,[3] the refectory,[4] a place for books,[5] the repository for clothes,[6] the kitchen, the larder,[7] the bakery,[8] the infirmary,[9] the workshops,[10] such as the forge, carpenter's shop, fuller's shop, tannery, shoemaker's shop,[11] and the houses into which the community was divided. The number of houses no doubt varied with the size of the monastery; Jerome speaks of thirty or forty in each. The houses, which seem to have consisted of twenty-two to forty monks,[12] contained small cells, one for each,[13] and a common room for meeting.[14] Near the door of the monastery was the house for the reception of strangers and friends of the monks; women were also admitted, but in a place carefully separated from the other sex.[15] The monastery also had its garden.[16]

The Government. All the monasteries were under the control of the Superior-General, or Archimandrite,[17] in whose hands lay the supreme power; he appointed the heads of the monasteries and transferred them from one to another, and regularly visited the various communities to lay down rules, advise, correct, and generally supervise.[18] He also named his successor.

---

[1] *Reg.*, 84; *Vit*, 29.   [2] *Reg. Præf.*, 3.   [3] *Reg.*, 1, etc.
[4] *Reg.*, 28; *H.L.*, 32.   [5] *Reg.*, 82, 100.
[6] *Reg*, 49, 70, 72, *Doctr. Orsis.*, 26.   [7] *Reg*, 41.
[8] *H L*, 32.   [9] *Reg*, 42, *Vit.*, 19.   [10] *Reg.*, 111.
[11] *H L*, 32.   [12] *Ep. Ammon.*, 4, 11; Jer, *Reg. Præf.*, 2.
[13] *Reg.*, 87, 89, 112, 114.   [14] *Reg.*, 181.
[15] *Reg*, 50, 51; *Vit*, 19.   [16] *Reg*, 73; *H.L*, 32.
[17] *Reg. Præf.*, 7; *H.L.*, 7.   [18] *Vit.*, 52, etc.

Each monastery was governed by its own superior, who had an assistant;[1] and the monks were divided into the houses, as far as possible according to their work,[2] each of which had its head and an assistant-head;[3] and a very high standard was required from those in authority.[4] Three or four houses formed a tribe;[5] one of the heads was also head of the tribe;[6] and each house had its own order of precedence.[7] The rank of a monk in his house was determined by his seniority as a member of the community.[8] Twice a year the monks went to Pabau, at Easter and on the 13th of August. The Easter assembly was held for the purpose of keeping the great Festival of the Resurrection in common. The August gathering was for administrative purposes, when official changes were made, and the superiors of the various monasteries gave an account of the work done during the year.[9] It was on this occasion that the striking scene took place when each forgave the wrongs done to him by others.[10]

The great idea of these regulations was to preserve the unity of the Pachomian institutions, which was further emphasised by the name, borne by all the followers of Pachomius, for after the place of its origin they were called "the monks of Tabennesis."[11]

Admission. All who came and were willing to obey the rules were admitted as members of the community, except those whose earlier life rendered them unsuitable.[12] There was no age limit, for Theodore became a

---

[1] *Reg.*, 8, 151 ff.; *Vit.*, 19; *Doctr. Orsis.*, 14.   [2] *Reg. Præf.*, 6.
[3] *Reg.*, 66, 181, 182, *Vit.* 19; *Doctr. Orsis*, 18.
[4] *Reg.* 159   [5] *Reg.*, 16; *Præf*, 2.   [6] *Reg.*, 115; *Vit.*, 19.
[7] *Reg.*, 59.   [8] *Reg. Præf.*, 3; cp. *Reg.*, 130.
[9] *Reg. Præf.*, 7, 8; *Reg.* 27; *Vit*, 52.
[10] *Reg.*, 27, *Ep Pach*, vii.   [11] *Vit*, 57; *Instit*, iv. 1, etc
[12] *Reg.*, 49.

Pachomian System

member of the community at the age of fourteen or fifteen,[1] another youth, Silvanus, was mentioned,[2] and there were regulations for the care of children.[3] Priests were admitted, but while no distinction as regards the rules was made between them and the rest, respect was shown for their office.[4] When a newcomer arrived seeking admission to the community, he had to remain for some days[5] outside the door of the monastery, under the care of the doorkeepers, who taught him prayers, psalms and the rules. He then received his new clothes and was taken to join the monks assembled for prayer.[6]

Dress. Each monk wore a linen tunic without sleeves, which was secured by a girdle, and came down to the knees, a goatskin, and around the neck a thin cape to which was attached a hood,[7] bearing the sign of the monastery and house.[8] He possessed also a staff, sandals for journeys (ordinarily he went barefooted), and a linen cloak which was worn only in the cell.[9] Those garments which were not used throughout the day were in the charge of the assistant-head of the house, so that no clothing, except that actually in use, was to be found in the cell.[10] The monks washed them at fixed times.[11] Garments were not to be left lying on the ground.[12] If a monk lost any garment, he received a reprimand and had to wait three weeks before it was replaced.[13] Cassian[14] found mystical meanings in the various articles of clothing, but the

---

[1] *Vit*, 18, 23. [2] *Vit*, 66. [3] *Reg*, 172-3.
[4] *Vit.*, 18. [5] Ten, according to *Instit.*, iv. 3.
[6] *Reg.*, 49; *Instit.*, iv. 5. [7] *Reg. Præf.*, 4; *Reg.*, 2.
[8] *Reg.*, 99. Palladius described the mark he saw as a cross worked in dark red (*H.L.*, 32).
[9] *Reg.*, 61, 81, 101. [10] *Reg.*, 66, 70, 72, *Vit.*, 38.
[11] *Reg.*, 67-71. [12] *Reg.*, 102, 148.
[13] *Reg.*, 131. [14] *Instit*, 1.

probability is that these garments were adopted for the sake of convenience, e.g. the hood was needed for the protection of the head in a hot country, the goatskin served for a wallet, and linen could be easily cleaned.

Divine Worship. The monks had prayers at dawn in each house,[1] and before returning to their cells they conferred on what they had heard.[2] At midday they met together for prayer,[3] and also in the evening for " six prayers ";[4] the latter would appear to have been " twelve prayers " in the time of Palladius.[5] Before they slept, they had in each house " six prayers and psalms,"[6] after which they returned to the cells and were not allowed to leave them.[7] Again, at night, they assembled for prayer.[8] The signal for the offices was given by those on duty for the week.[9] The superior of the monastery presided at the services, which consisted of psalms, prayers and lessons.[10] The lessons were recited by heart by those on duty for the week.[11] No monk could be present in sandals,[12] but he had to wear the cape and goatskin.[13] The Eucharist was celebrated on Saturdays and Sundays,[14] and in the early days before clergy joined the community a priest was obtained from a neighbouring church.[15] The hours of prayer were observed by the monks wherever they were—in a boat, or in the field, or on a journey;[16] they were, moreover, expected to meditate on their way to and from the cells,[17] and at their work.[18]

---

[1] *Reg.*, 20 ; cf. *Vit.*, 39. Perhaps, at an earlier period, it was a general gathering, according to Boh. and Sahid , *Annales*, pp. 171, 318.

[2] *Reg.*, 20. [3] *Reg.*, 24. [4] *Reg*, 24 ; cf. 121, 155.
[5] *H.L.*, 32 [6] *Reg.*, 155, 186.
[7] *Reg.*, 126 [8] *Reg.*, 10. [9] *Reg.*, 24 [10] *Reg*, 8.
[11] *Reg.*, 13. [12] *Reg*, 101. [13] *Reg*, 91. [14] *H L.*, 32.
[15] *Vit.*, 18. [16] *Reg*, 142. [17] *Reg*, 3, 28.
[18] *Reg.*, 36, 37, 60.

Pachomian System

Education. On the bi-weekly fast days instruction was given to his monks by the head of the house,[1] at which attendance was obligatory,[2] and to all by the superior of the monastery.[3] Pachomius used to instruct his monks on Christian doctrine and the Scriptures,[4] and for a long time Theodore was in the habit of going daily in the evening to Pabau to hear him.[5] Great emphasis was laid on the study and the learning by heart of the Scriptures.[6] Those who could not read had to learn, and received lessons at the first, third and sixth hours;[7] and books could be borrowed.[8] Discussions of a spiritual character were also held by the monks, especially on fast days,[9] after morning prayer,[10] and in the evenings when work was ended.[11]

Work. A common occupation of the monks was the weaving of rushes into mats and baskets; and oil was allowed for the hands, after manual labour.[12] An example of work was to be set by the superiors of the monasteries,[13] but excessive toil was not commended.[14] Many were occupied with special work, which naturally increased with the size of the community. Thus mention is made of those who were responsible for the cooking,[15] prepared the tables in the refectory,[16] served at meals,[17] had care of the sick,[18] of those at the door who received strangers and prepared new members,[19] of those in charge of clothes,[20] of makers of linen and mats, menders of old garments, carpenters, fullers,

---

[1] *Reg.*, 115, 138, 156. [2] *Reg*, 188. [3] *Reg.*, 22.
[4] *Vit.*, 36. [5] *Vit*, 56. [6] e.g. *H.L.*, 32.
[7] *Reg.*, 139, 140. [8] *Reg*, 100, 144. [9] *Reg.*, 138.
[10] *Reg.*, 20. [11] *Vit.*, 79; cf. *Reg.*, 122. [12] *Reg*, 92.
[13] *Reg*, 177; cf *Vit*, 33, 45. [14] *Reg*, 179.
[15] *Reg*, 44, 116, 117. [16] *H.L*, 32. [17] *Reg*, 33.
[18] *Reg*, 40, 129; *Vit.*, 19. [19] *Reg*, 49, 51; *Vit*, 19.
[20] *Reg.*, 49.

shoemakers,[1] sailors, millers,[2] herdsmen, those engaged in agriculture[3] and in the garden.[4] Palladius says[5] that he saw in the monastery of Panopolis fifteen tailors, seven smiths, four carpenters, twelve cameldrivers, and fifteen fullers. Pigs too were seen there. The *Vita Pachomii* (81) also states that under Orsisius agricultural work was developed. During work the rule of silence was observed,[6] or at least they abstained from worldly conversation;[7] sometimes, however, they sang psalms, and they were expected to meditate constantly on the Scriptures. Each house in turn was on duty for a week to supply the general service for the community, and if the numbers were not sufficient, the head used to ask for help from others of the same tribe.[8] They called the monks to the offices and meals,[9] conveyed the orders of the superior for the day to those concerned,[10] obtained the quantity of rushes asked for on the previous night by the heads of houses, moistened them, distributed them in the morning,[11] and accompanied any brother who had to work outside the monastery, carrying his food and drink.[12] At the end of the week the chief of those on duty with the superior of the monastery kept an account of the week's work, which the latter rendered to the chief steward at the August meeting at Pabau.[13] Occasionally the monks went down the Nile to Alexandria to buy and sell, for which purpose two boats were owned by the community.[14]

Pachomius's aim in giving manual work to his monks was twofold: it was essential for their main-

[1] *Reg. Præf.*, 6. [2] *Reg.*, 67. [3] *Reg*, 108
[4] *Reg.*, 73. [5] *H.L.*, 32. [6] *Reg*, 68, 116.
[7] *Reg*, 60. [8] *Reg*, 15; *Vit.*, 19. [9] *Reg.*, 24, 36.
[10] *Reg.*, 25. [11] *Reg.*, 26 [12] *Reg*, 64
[13] *Reg. Præf.*, 6; *Reg.*, 27, *Vit.*, 52. [14] *Vit.*, 73.

Pachomian System

tenance, but he also realised its spiritual advantage. But as time passed, the increase in numbers was necessarily accompanied by the development of work and the consequent growth of wealth. This was not to the advantage of the community, as we see in the schism which nearly occurred a few years after the death of Pachomius.

Food. The monks ordinarily ate together in the refectory at fixed hours.[1] There were two meals daily, the first at midday,[2] and the second in the evening.[3] Some, however, came only to one meal, or ate very little at supper, while others received food in their cells, consisting of bread, salt and water.[4] This corresponds with *Vit.*, 19,[5] where it is stated that opportunities were given for living a more ascetic mode of life ; indeed, it appeared to a visitor as if the common meals were but a formality, for they ate very little of what was on the table.[6] Still, others were able to have what their work, age or infirmity required ;[7] and Theodore discouraged excessive asceticism on the ground that it rendered the monks unable to perform properly their devotions and work.[8] At meals each was barefooted,[9] wore his sheepskin and cape,[10] occupied his own appointed place,[11] with head covered by the hood,[12] ate in silence,[13] and took no notice of others.[14] If he wanted anything, he would give a signal to the attendant.[15] On leaving the refectory, he was given sweetmeats called *tragemata*,[16]

---

[1] *Reg Præf*, 5, *Reg*, 8, 29, 36–7, 90, *Vit*, 34, 71.
[2] *Reg. Præf*, 5, cf *Vit*, 43.
[3] *Reg Præf*, 5 ; *Vit*, 49   [4] *Reg. Præf*, 5, *Reg*, 80.
[5] cf *H L*, 32.   [6] *H M.*, 3.   [7] *Reg Præf*, 5.
[8] *Ep. Ammon*, 13.   [9] *Reg.*, 101.   [10] *Reg*, 91.
[11] *Reg.*, 29, 30   [12] *Reg*, 29
[13] *Reg.*, 31, *Instit.* iv. 17 ; *H.M.*, 3.   [14] *Reg.*, 30 ; *H.L.*, 32.
[15] *Reg*, 33.   [16] *Reg*, 37.

sufficient for three days;[1] otherwise he could not have even the poorest apples in his cell.[2] The food consisted of bread, cheese, herbs, charlock, preserved olives, and fruit,[3] but neither wine[4] nor meat.[5] The head of the house gave instruction to his monks on behaviour at meals.[6]

In the time of Pachomius the Wednesday and Friday fasts were observed by the heads of houses, but not by the whole community;[7] later, however, these fasts were observed by the monks generally, except at Easter and Pentecost.[8] During Lent they were said to use only uncooked food, while some ate only every two or five days.[9]

Illness. The sick monk was taken by the head of his house to the infirmary,[10] where he was given all that his condition required,[11] including wine[12] and meat,[13] if he chose.[14] Similar care was shown if he did not wish to go to the infirmary.[15] No one could visit him without permission.[16] A monk who was taken ill on a journey was allowed to eat food ordinarily forbidden, but not in the presence of those who accompanied him.[17] When a brother died, all were present at the last rites.[18]

Sleep. The amount of sleep actually taken between "the six prayers" and midnight[19] was left to the individual, and we know that some observed long vigils.[20] Pillows were not allowed.[21] In the great heat they could sleep on the roofs.[22] After retiring, they were not allowed to speak with one another or to leave

---

[1] *Reg.*, 39. [2] *Reg.*, 114. [3] *Vit.*, 35; *H L.*, 32
[4] *Reg*, 45. [5] *Vit*, 34. [6] *Reg.*, 31.
[7] *Vit.*, 19. [8] *Reg. Præf.*, 5. [9] *H.L.*, 18.
[10] *Reg.*, 42. [11] *Reg Præf*, 5. [12] *Reg*, 45.
[13] *Vit.*, 34. [14] *Vit*, 50. [15] *Reg*, 40, 105.
[16] *Reg.*, 42, 47. [17] *Reg*, 46. [18] *Reg.*, 127–9.
[19] *Reg.*, 126. [20] *Vit.*, 67. [21] *Reg.*, 81. [22] *Reg.*, 87.

their cells;[1] and the doors of the cells were left open.[2] If they awoke during the night, they prayed.[3]

Punishment. The monks were under constant observation and correction.[4] Those who talked, laughed, or were late at the offices, stood with head bent before the altar, received reproof, and had to undergo further penance at the meal.[5] For similar offences at meals a monk was corrected, and had to stand, or return foodless.[6] If a monk lost anything, he was publicly admonished before the altar.[7] He who slept during the instruction of the head of the house, or of the superior, had to stand.[8] Cases of lying, disobedience, laziness, etc., were dealt with by the superior of the monastery.[9] After repeated warnings had been given according to the nature of his offence, various other punishments were in vogue : living on bread and water for seven days was given to detractors,[10] murmurers, and complainers at work underwent the humiliating experience of being sent to the infirmary;[11] those who gave way to anger were degraded, took the lowest places in the assemblies, and on their repentance were required to have three sponsors;[12] corporal punishment was given to perverters of souls[13] and to children;[14] and finally, there was expulsion.[15] Novel offences, for which no punishment was stated, were reported to the superior of the monastery.[16] Likewise, to him the escape of a monk was to be reported immediately; otherwise the head of the house was considered responsible.[17] Heads of houses were bound to correct

---

[1] *Reg*, 126. [2] *Reg.*, 107. [3] *Reg*, 87
[4] *Vit*, 27, 41, 85. [5] *Reg.*, 8, 9. [6] *Reg.*, 31, 32.
[7] *Reg*, 131. [8] *Reg*, 22. [9] *Reg.*, 151.
[10] *Reg*, 160. [11] *Reg*, 164. [12] *Reg*, 161
[13] *Reg.*, 163; cf *Instit.*, iv 16. [14] *Reg.*, 173.
[15] *Ep Ammon.*, 12, 16; *Instit.*, iv. 16. [16] *Reg*, 133.
[17] *Reg.*, 153.

when it was necessary;[1] and complaints against a head could be brought by all the monks of the house to the superior,[2] but in the latter's absence, the case could be heard by monks of high reputation.[3]

General features. The wise regulations of the Pachomian system aimed at equal treatment for all and a united community,[4] and no one was allowed to take advantage of his office.[5] But the features that marked the originality of Pachomius were the common life, the mildness of the rules, and the emphasis laid on obedience. No excess was desired,[6] for Pachomius wished all to be able to perform their duties; even a fire was lighted in the cold weather.[7] This leniency was extended also to their relations, for a monk could, by the permission of the superior and the head of the house, visit sick relations, or attend their funerals, and receive visits from relations, on the understanding that, when absent, he ate only what was allowed in the monastery, and that no news of the outside world was to be brought in;[8] but no one was allowed to go alone.[9] Obedience received a new significance in monasticism, to which in the cenobitic life great importance was attached;[10] and it is scarcely necessary to add that the rules of chastity and poverty were observed by all. The conversation of the monks was always to be spiritual;[11] they were not allowed to carry news from house to house or from one monastery to another,[12] and they had to be careful in their relations with one another,[13] and to avoid laughing and

---

[1] *Reg.*, 154.   [2] *Reg.*, 158.   [3] *Reg.*, 190.
[4] *Reg.*, 35, 40, 80, 97, 179.   [5] *Reg.*, 39, 41, 76–8.
[6] *Reg.*, 179; *H.L.*, 32.   [7] *Reg.*, 5, 23, 120; *Vit.*, 39.
[8] *Reg.*, 52, 53, 55, 57, 86.   [9] *Reg.*, 56.
[10] *Reg.*, 3, 11, 23, 30, 58, 103, 123–4, 157, 167, 194, *Vit.*, 19, 38.
[11] *Reg.*, 60, 122.   [12] *Reg.*, 85–6.   [13] *Reg.*, 93–95, 109.

Pachomian System

playing with the younger.[1] But there is no ground for Amélineau's belief in the want of chastity on the part of the Pachomian monks; Ladeuze[2] has dealt with the matter at some length and shown the baselessness of such charges.

Foreigners. Jerome states that a large number of Latins were to be found in the monasteries of the Thebaid;[3] and we are informed by the *Vita Pachomii* (60) and *Ep. Ammon.* (4) that at Pabau there was a special house for Greeks, Romans and foreigners, of which Theodore the Alexandrian was head and Ausonius the second.

Numbers. The writers are in general agreement as to the number of monks, if the exaggerations of Jerome be put on one side, who said there were 50,000 in 404.[4] According to Palladius[5] there were 3000 during the lifetime of Pachomius; c. 350, after the losses incurred by the pestilence, Ammon says (13) that there were "more than 2000," while at the time that Palladius wrote (c. 420), there were 7000,[6] and Cassian[7] gives the estimate of "more than 5000." The ordinary number at each monastery was 200 to 300;[8] but Pabau was larger, for in c. 350 there were 600,[9] which had increased to 1300 or 1400 at the beginning of the fifth century.[10]

Relations with other monks. The relations between Pachomian and other monks appear to have been friendly and cordial, and there was a general spirit of comradeship between them. At the Pachomian monasteries, in the earlier days at least, the feet of visiting monks were washed, and although they were

---

[1] *Reg*, 166.   [2] pp. 327 ff.   [3] *Reg. Præf.*, 1.
[4] *Reg. Præf.*, 7   [5] *H.L.*, 7.   [6] *H L.*, 32.
[7] *Instit.*, IV 1.   [8] *H L*, 32.   [9] *Ep Ammon.*, 1.
[10] *H.L.*, 18, 32.

obliged to eat and sleep in the guest-house, they were allowed to be present at the offices.[1] Pachomius himself regarded Anthony as one of the three great marvels of his age.[2] Anthony bore witness to the greatness of the work of Pachomius, and said that his wish to meet him had not come to pass.[3] Pachomian monks visited Anthony, who gave them a commendatory letter for Athanasius.[4] Anthony also wrote to Theodore.[5] We have already seen that monks in the neighbourhood joined the Pachomian monasteries. There was too a certain intercourse with the monks of Nitria, for Theodore wrote a letter to them,[6] Arsisius of Nitria knew Pachomius,[7] and Macarius of Alexandria and Ammon were for a time Tabennesiot monks.[8]

iii. White Monastery

A further great figure of Egyptian monastic history was Schenoudi, who developed the cenobitic life on somewhat different lines from Pachomius. It is a curious fact that he is not mentioned by any Greek or Latin writer, not even by Palladius, who visited and described in some detail the Pachomian monastery at Panopolis only a few miles away from Schenoudi's monastery. The reason is that he wrote and spoke in Sahidic Coptic, and our knowledge of him is derived from modern discoveries of Coptic MSS.

He was born at Schenalolet in c. 333–4 if he really attained the great age of one hundred and eighteen years. His father was not well off, but he owned some sheep and arable land, and possibly had the assistance

[1] *Reg.*, 51; *Vit*, 28.   [2] *Vit.*, 87.   [3] *Vit*, 77.
[4] *Vit.*, 77.   [5] *Ep. Ammon*, 20.
[6] *Ep. Ammon*, 22.   [7] *H L.*, 7.
[8] *H.L.*, 18; *Ep. Ammon.*, Prol.

White Monastery

of a shepherd.[1] As a young boy he went to live with his maternal uncle, Bgoul, the head of the White Monastery near Atripe on the western bank of the Nile, nearly opposite Panopolis,[2] where he won such a position of authority that by Bgoul's wish he succeeded him on his death. This happened not later than 385, for correspondence passed between Schenoudi and Archbishop Timothy, who died in that year, on the subject of his succession. There are very few important events recorded of his life, but he was present at the Council of Ephesus in 431, and died c. 451.[3] The main sphere of his activity and the development of the community therefore belong to the fifth century, but his place in a survey of Egyptian monasticism to 400 A.D. cannot be wholly ignored, for he was head of his monastery for some fifteen years in the fourth century, and his rules were based on those of Bgoul; and under these circumstances it will suffice to point out the chief characteristics of his system.

During his administration the monastery increased greatly in importance and size; large numbers came to him, and new buildings had to be built as well as a convent for nuns, and we are told that he came to rule over twenty-two thousand monks and eighteen thousand nuns, but whether that be so or not a very large number was subject to his authority.[4] This famous Coptic Christian was strong both mentally and physically, possessed the gift of eloquence, was a stern administrator, did much for the relief of the poor,[5] was distinguished for his care of souls, was a great lover of his country and took an enthusiastic part in

[1] *M.*, 3, 633. [2] *M.*, 5 ff.
[3] Leipoldt, *Schenute*, 41 ff; Ladeuze, 241 ff.
[4] *M.*, 230 ff., 331. [5] e g *M.*, 18, 42, 244 f., 648.

the popular movement against heathenism and in the destruction of temples.[1] He was, however, passionately fond of power, self-confident and ruled his monks with an iron hand. Nevertheless, he was held in the highest esteem by the inhabitants of the neighbourhood[2] and the officials.[3] Bgoul's rules[4] have not come down to us; although they were stricter,[5] they were founded upon the rules of Pachomius;[6] but they were probably few in number, for Schenoudi enlarged them by many long letters.[7]

Features of the White Monastery. It was essentially a Coptic institution, where the Sahidic dialect was used. The head of the whole community was designated the Father, and was known in the fifth century as the Archimandrite, who was assisted by a secretary.[8] On his admission each monk promised in writing to obey the rules,[9] and so the position of the Father was strengthened in any case of dispute. There were two meals a day, at midday[10] and in the evening,[11] but the monks were expected to partake of only one.[12] Two occupied each cell, which was divided into two compartments by a wall[13] On Saturdays and Sundays the Divine services were attended by the people of the neighbourhood.[14] Special honour was paid to the dead, and their names were placed on a tablet[15] At the White Monastery there seems to have been some attempt to combine the advantages of the eremitical and the cenobitic life, for at times Schenoudi and other monks used to depart to cells in the desert.[16] And,

---

[1] e.g. *M*, 45 f, 66, 238, 240
[2] *M.*, 25, 30, 38.
[3] *M*, 57, 70, 642 f
[4] *M*, 229
[5] *M*, 236.
[6] *M*, 235, Zoega, 212, 230.
[7] *M*, 87
[8] *M.*, 65
[9] *M.*, 234.
[10] *M.*, 267.
[11] *M*, 281
[12] *M*, 8, 236, 415.
[13] *M*, 253 f.
[14] *M.*, 647, 398, 433.
[15] *M.*, 278.
[16] *M*, 20, 65, 75, 637.

Other Monasteries

lastly, it was a community governed with great strictness and harshness; imprisonment and corporal punishment were in vogue, and on one occasion so severe was the flogging administered by Schenoudi himself that a monk died as the result;[1] and monks were frequently expelled.[2] It was a hard system, which did not make for love or affection, but no doubt the large numbers necessitated a stern hand on the part of the ruler, and Schenoudi by his unique personality, his fearlessness, and hardness, was able to enforce the rules and maintain discipline.

iv. Other Cenobitic Monasteries

There is evidence, however, of other cenobitic establishments in Egypt besides those of Pachomius and Schenoudi. They are mentioned by the author of *Historia Monachorum* as well as Cassian, who did not visit Upper Egypt, and the latter discussed their advantages over the solitary life, while Jerome, in 384, wrote a short account of such communities.[3]

The *Historia Monachorum* refers to two such monasteries. Apollo, who formerly lived in a cave with five disciples, became the head of a large monastery, containing five hundred monks, near Hermopolis, who had a common table and partook of the Eucharist daily at the ninth hour before their meal. On the arrival of expected visitors the monks went out to meet them, singing psalms, for such was the custom with all the brethren, and having bowed down with their faces to the ground, they kissed them. Then they proceeded together, some in front and others behind, singing

---

[1] Leipoldt, op. cit., 140 ff. [2] *M.*, 54, *Zoega*, 212.
[3] *Ep.*, 22.

psalms until they reached Apollo. He also bowed low to the earth, kissed the visitors, led them in, and after prayer washed their feet and invited them to rest, and this he was accustomed to do to all the brethren who came to him. At their meal the monks listened to his teaching, and afterwards some would go out to the desert and repeat the Scriptures all night, others would remain and sing hymns through the night until daybreak. Many for days lived only on the food of the Eucharist; but in spite of such austerities it was a very joyful community.[1]

Also Isidore, in the Thebaid, had a monastery which was a strong building with a high brick wall containing a very large number of monks, who did not go outside but had wells, gardens and all the necessaries of life within; only two monks were allowed to go outside for the purpose of buying and selling, and a doorkeeper, who prevented any from going out or coming in, had a small house by the gate, where strangers were lodged for the night.[2]

The cenobitic monasteries mentioned by Cassian appear to have been situated in or near the Delta. At Diolcos a large number lived the cenobitic life.[3] Pinufius was the abbot and presbyter of a huge establishment not far from Panephysis;[4] John presided over a large monastery near Thmuis;[5] over two hundred monks lived this mode of life under Paul;[6] and Patermucius joined a similar monastery with his little boy, and soon became its abbot[7]

They probably were indebted to the Pachomian example, but they were less strictly organised,[8] and

[1] H.M., 8 [2] H.M., 19.
[3] Instit., v. 36; Soz., H.E., vi. 29.
[4] Instit., iv. 30; Coll., xx. 1. [5] Coll., xiv. 4.
[6] Coll., xix. 1. [7] Instit., iv. 27 l. [8] Instit., iv. 1.

Other Monasteries

began in a very small way with eight or ten monks.[1] Some knowledge of this monasticism can be derived from the pages of Cassian as well as from Jerome. The head of the cenobium must be a monk experienced in the life, wise, humble and who had learned obedience.[2] Mention is made in one case of the abbot's cell, which he had built in the furthest corner of the monastery garden.[3] The monks were divided into bodies of ten under leaders (decani), and a hundred, over whom was a higher officer, and it was the duty of the decani to visit and comfort those who were in trouble.[4]

To become a monk it was necessary to lie at the entrance for ten days with tears, after which the suitable candidate was admitted. On the occasion of his admission an address was given to him by the abbot.[5] According to Cassian,[6] the dress of Egyptian monks generally consisted of a linen tunic, a cord, a narrow cape for the neck and shoulders, a robe which was to be neither very different from the ordinary nor very fashionable, a hood such as was worn by children, a girdle and a sheepskin. They used to carry a staff and wear sandals if necessary, but these were removed for the Eucharist. On their journeys all monks were in the habit of carrying a scrip as well as a staff.[7] There were only two daily services, Vespers and the night office, for the monks otherwise spent the whole day in their cells at work and prayer. But they assembled together for their offices, consisting of twelve psalms, each being followed by a short prayer, and two lessons, one from the Old and the other from the New Testament, except on Saturdays and Sundays and from

---

[1] *Coll.*, vii. 23. [2] *Instit.*, ii. 3. [3] *Coll*, xx 2.
[4] Jer., *Ep.*, xxii. 35. [5] *Instit.*, iv. 32 ff.; *Coll.*, xx. 2.
[6] *Instit.*, 1. [7] *Coll.*, xi. 3.

Easter to Whitsuntide, when both lessons were taken from the New.[1] A peculiarity of Egyptian monasticism was the method of singing the psalms; they were divided between two, three or at most four brothers, who recited their sections in turn, so that while one sang the others sat, except at the Gloria, when all stood.[2] Long psalms were broken up by prayers interspersed, and if an inexperienced singer forgot this he was stopped by the superior clapping his hands.[3] They sat in very low stalls, and the reason why they were allowed to sit during the psalms was that they were worn out by fasting and working during the day and the vigils by night.[4] It was not their custom to kneel or fast from Saturday evening to Sunday evening, or from Easter to Whitsuntide.[5] On Saturdays and Sundays they met together at the third hour for the Holy Communion,[6] and Sundays were wholly spent in prayer and reading [7] After the night office each returned without loitering or gossiping to his cell and spent the night in vigil, repeating the same service of prayer with greater earnestness as his special private sacrifice.[8]

The monks were engaged in incessant manual work. Each had his own cell, which was sometimes shared by one other on account of partnership in work or training, or of similarity of disposition. They were not allowed to leave their cells or cease work during the day, except for special reasons, and importance was attached to the repetition of Scripture during work so that minds as well as hands might be occupied.[9]

---

[1] *Instit.*, ii. 4, 6 f.; iii. 2; Jer, *Ep*, xxii. 35.
[2] *Instit*, ii. 8, 11.   [3] *Instit*, ii. 11.   [4] *Instit*, ii. 12.
[5] *Instit.*, ii. 18.   [6] *Instit.*, iii. 2.   [7] Jer., *Ep.*, xxii. 35.
[8] *Instit.*, ii. 12, 15; iii. 5
[9] *Instit.*, ii. 12, 14, 15; iii. 2; Jer., *Ep.*, xxii. 35.

Various duties were assigned to approved monks : for example, one was appointed to summon the others to the offices, and in order to ascertain the right hours for service he was advised to study the course of the stars.[1] In these monasteries a permanent cook was appointed, and held this office as long as his strength and years permitted.[2] It was the steward's duty to taste the dishes when they were cooked.[3] Other monks served at table.[4] To the steward the monks reported on or brought their work daily[5] through the decani, and the steward rendered a monthly account to the superior.[6] There was an almoner, chosen for his age, probity and suitability, to whom tithes were brought by the faithful.[7] Mention is also made of a guest-chamber and an infirmary.[8] After the needs of the monastery were satisfied, the products of the monks' work were distributed by the abbot among the poor and the prisons.[9]

No monk was allowed to stop or go about with another or to hold another's hands in his. This was a strict rule, especially with the younger monks. For a breach of it, public penance was required in the presence of all the brethren, otherwise such an offender was not allowed to be present at the public offices.[10] Cells were visited during the night, and ears were placed against the doors to discover what the occupants were doing. If a monk was found to be slothful in his vigils, he was visited more frequently rather than scolded.[11] Although a kindly discipline seems generally to have prevailed, an instance is given when a monk who was slow in serving was given a blow by

---

[1] *Instit.*, ii. 17.   [2] *Instit.*, iv. 22.   [3] Jer., *Ep.*, xxii. 35.
[4] *Coll.*, xix. 1.   [5] *Instit.*, x 20.   [6] Jer., *Ep.*, xxii. 35.
[7] *Coll.*, xxi. 1, 9.   [8] *Coll.*, xviii. 7.   [9] *Coll.*, xviii. 7.
[10] *Instit.*, ii. 15.   [11] Jer., *Ep.*, xxii. 35.

the abbot's hand so heavy that it was heard at some distance.¹ But they were not allowed to eat even fruit, except at meals. At the common meal each body of ten had its own table ;² silence was observed, hoods were drawn over the eyes so that they could see only the table and the food thereon.³ Bread, pulse and greens seasoned with salt formed their ordinary fare.⁴ Dried and uncooked food was mostly eaten, and Cassian adds that leaves of leeks, charlock, table salt; olives and tiny salt fish were esteemed the greatest delicacies.⁵ But special meals were often provided for children and the old.⁶ At the festival of the anniversary of an abbot's death great numbers from other cenobia were present and had their meal in the large open court, divided into parties of twelve ⁷

v. *Communities of Women*

In the early Church the virgins occupied an important place ; but they lived in the world and resided at home. Mention, however, is made of a parthenon in Egypt (*c.* 270),⁸ and of one which numbered seventy virgins.⁹ But the monastic life for women only grew up after it had been adopted by men. The solitary life was followed by some,¹⁰ but obviously the difficulties and dangers of the desert rendered it unsuitable for women.

The first community was founded by Pachomius ; for one day Mary, his sister, came to pay him a visit at Tabennesis ; he, however, sent a message to the effect

---

[1] *Coll*, xix. 1.
[2] Jer, *Ep*, xxii. 35.
[3] *Instit*, iv 17 f., v 20
[4] Jer, *Ep*, xxii 35
[5] *Instit*, iv 22
[6] Jer., *Ep.*, xxii. 35.
[7] *Coll*, xix 1.
[8] *Vit Ant*, 3.
[9] *H.L*, 1.
[10] *H.L.*, 5, 11, 29.

Communities of Women

that he was unable to see her, but was willing to build her a dwelling. This offer was tearfully accepted, and the brethren built a cell for her in the village at some distance from the monastery. Soon the fame of this new venture spread, and many women came and placed themselves under her direction,[1] amongst whom was the mother of Theodore, after she had failed to persuade her son to return home.[2] Pachomius gave rules for the community which were similar to those of the monks. An old monk, Peter, was appointed to visit it; and if any building work was required by the women, it was done by the monks, who were obliged always to return for their meals. But if a monk had a sister or near relation in the convent, he could visit her, accompanied by a senior brother and in the presence of the head.[3]

A second community for women was established later by Pachomius in the neighbourhood of the monastery at Tismenæ or Men; and under the administration of Theodore a third community grew up near Pabau, in the village of Bechre.[4] Of one of them, possibly Tismenæ, Palladius[5] said that there were four hundred women, and described their method of burial; when a nun died, her body was taken down to the river-side and there left until the monks came across, took the body with them in the boat, and then buried it.[6] He also added that only the priest and the deacon were allowed to go to the convent—on Sundays. Part of the surplus of the monks' work went to provide for the needs of the convents.[7]

Mention has already been made of the convent

---

[1] *Vit. Pach*, 22. [2] *Vit. Pach.*, 26. [3] *Vit Pach*, 22
[4] *Vit. Pach*, 86. [5] *H.L*, 33 [6] cf. *Vit. Pach.*, 22.
[7] *H.L*, 32.

which was founded by Schenoudi, and was said to consist of eighteen hundred women. The head of it was known as the mother, and the father of the monastery and the mother of the convent dealt with the affairs of the women by correspondence.[1]

Palladius also wrote of other convents. At Antinoë there were twelve, over one of which the aged Amatalis presided; she had been an ascetic for eighty years and was greatly beloved by her nuns, who included a virgin named Taor, that had been resident there for thirty years. These nuns went to church on the Lord's Day for Communion.[2] Not far from Schenoudi's convent there was another, consisting of three hundred, at Athribe, which Elias had founded and managed, of whom it is said " he had compassion on the class of women ascetics, and having property in the city of Athribe built a great monastery and brought into the monastery all the dispersed women, caring for them consistently (with his purpose) and procured them every kind of refreshment, and gardens and utensils, and whatever their life required."[3] Chrysostom also refers to associations of virgins in Egypt;[4] and the *Historia Monachorum* (5) states that there were very many nuns at Oxyrhynchus.

[1] *Zoega*, 212.
[2] *H L*, 59.
[3] *H.L.*, 29.
[4] *Hom. in Matt*, c. 8.

IV

ASPECTS OF EGYPTIAN MONASTICISM

1. Sacrifices of the Monks

THE great ideal of monasticism was the eager desire to seek direct personal intercourse with God away from the pollutions and hindrances of the world. For this purpose purity of heart was the great necessity, and austerity of life was the means by which it was to be sought.[1] The intense spirit of sacrifice was the ascetic answer to the call of Christ: "If any man would come after Me, let him deny himself, and take up his cross and follow Me."

To achieve these ideals, no refusal of the comforts and pleasures of life was too great. Heron[2] even went so far in his austerities as to be almost branded a suicide; and there are some indications of that craving for excessive austerities, which were found in the East, for Ammonius,[3] to repress carnal thoughts, put red-hot irons on his members, and Pachon deliberately incited an asp to bite him.[4] Such practices, however, were hardly characteristic of Egyptian monasticism as a whole, but the attitude of Dorotheus towards the body represented too common a tendency, expressed by him in the extreme saying: "It kills me,

---

[1] *Coll.*, 1. 7, 22; xxi. 15; *Instit.*, v. 22.
[2] *Coll.*, 11. 5.   [3] *H.L.*, 11.   [4] *H.L.*, 23.

Christian Monasticism in Egypt

I kill it."[1] The austerities that were practised were found mainly in the severe limitation of food and sleep, simplicity in dress, the burden of the sheep or goatskin under a hot sun, the repression of the sexual instinct, the neglect of family, the rejection of the bath and oil for anointing, and even abstention from spitting.[2]

The Egyptians in their religion had laid great stress upon bodily cleanliness, and little importance was attached to the idea of ethical purity.[3] But with the rise of a new ethical ideal, the unclean bodily habits of the monks represented a reaction from mere formal ablutions, and emphasized in an extreme manner the need for inward as opposed to outward purity; even a love of dirt was frankly confessed;[4] and in the words of Sozomen[5]: "By purity of soul and by a life of good works they entered without guilt upon religious observances, and despised purifications, lustral vessels, and such ceremonials; for they think that sins alone are blemishes."

The sacrifices of the monk included also the neglect of his family, for "remembrance of kinsfolk" was the work of evil spirits.[6] So the address at the admission of a new monk bade him remember nothing of his kinsfolk;[7] provision for monks on the part of relations was condemned;[8] Apollos refused to help his brother rescue an ox because he had been "dead to this world for twenty years";[9] another after an interval of fifteen years received a bundle of letters from his parents and friends, but burnt them unread because they would have disturbed his thoughts;[10] and the fate is described that befell one who endeavoured to

---

[1] *H.L*, 2.   [2] *H.L*, 18.   [3] *H D B.*, v 192; *E.R.E.*, v. 482.
[4] *Coll.*, iv. 11.   [5] *H E.*, 1 12   [6] *Vit Ant*, 36.
[7] *Instit.*, iv. 36.   [8] *Coll.*, xxiv 11.   [9] *Coll*, xxiv. 9.
[10] *Instit.*, v. 32

return and save his wife and only son.¹ But this attitude was carried even to such lengths that a father, who was admitted to a monastery with his son, was obliged, as a test, to see him cruelly ill-treated, and indeed to cast him with his own hands into the river;² and Theonas deserted his wife against her will, an action which was approved by many.³

A noteworthy feature of Egyptian life was its looseness in sexual matters.⁴ Consequently when monasticism held up the necessity of abstinence from marriage and all sexual relations, it was a lofty ideal for Egyptians with their old traditions and habits; and so stern was the conflict that the early records of monasticism are crowded with the subject of chastity and the difficulties of self-control. Indeed, so fierce were the temptations that the life of chastity assumed the aspect of a romance; and those who entered the conflict were engaged in a great adventure, which was attractive to the Egyptians by its novelty and its strenuousness.⁵ The importance attached to celibacy frequently carried with it an absurd attitude towards women; Pachomius refused to see his sister when she came to visit him; Pior⁶ after fifty years visited his sister by her desire, and during the interview kept his eyes shut; Paul⁷ one day met a woman by chance, neglected the business he was doing, and "dashed back again to his monastery with greater speed than a man would flee from the face of a lion or terrible dragon," in spite of the shouts and prayers of his companion Archebius. However, in later years he

---
¹ Sulp., *Dial.*, 1. 22.   ² *Instit*, iv. 27.   ³ *Coll*, xxi. 9 f.
⁴ *E R E*, v 482, 733; Erman, *Life in Ancient Egypt*, 154 f.; E A W. Budge, *Osiris*, ii 213 f.
⁵ cf H Ellis, *Psychology of Sex*, vi. 151 ff   ⁶ *H L*, 39.
⁷ *Coll.*, vii. 26.

became so paralysed that by the irony of circumstances his condition necessitated women's care, and he was taken to a community of virgins. On the other hand, an amusing picture is drawn by Palladius[1] of Dorotheus, who managed the affairs of a convent, and shutting himself in an upper chamber, kept his watch on the women from the window, although the founder of the community[2] had lived near them.

Complete renunciation of possessions proved a very difficult ideal to the monks, for some tried to get too much money for their work, or had three or four tunics instead of two, while others possessed huts with four or five cells, large and splendidly decorated.[3]

But with the inauguration of the cenobitic life a further form of sacrifice came into prominence—the surrender of the will, or obedience.[4] This might involve the performance of things that were either foolish or humiliating, and it was more than some could endure.[5] Cassian relates that many unable to make this surrender came to be known as Sarabaites, who "have broken away from the congregation of the cenobites," and unwilling to practise obedience live two or three in a cell together, "wander where they will and do what they like," shirked severities, and laid up money for themselves.[6] Jerome[7] has a somewhat similar account of such monks in Egypt, whom he calls Remoboth, and says that they live mostly in cities, "compete with each other in fasting, in everything they study effect . . . are always sighing, or visiting virgins, or sneering at the clergy."

But while renunciation of the world dominated

---

[1] *H.L.*, 30. [2] *H L.*, 29. [3] *Coll*, ix 5, cf. *Instit.*, vii. 7.
[4] *Instit.*, ii 3; iv., 1 ff.; Sulpit., *Dial.*, i. 18.
[5] *Instit.*, iv. 24 ff., 29; *Coll.*, iv. 20. [6] *Coll.*, xviii. 7.
[7] *Ep*, xxii. 34

monastic thought, a loftier view of that relation was not unknown : " There is no village nor city in Egypt and the Thebaid which is not surrounded by monasteries as if by walls, and the inhabitants are supported by their prayers as if resting on God ";[1] and a like saying of Macarius the Alexandrian has been preserved, " for Christ's sake, I am guarding the walls."[2]

2. Social and Intellectual Status of the Monks

Great emphasis is often laid upon the ignorance and low origin of the monks, but it would be more true to describe monasticism as a great popular movement, for the life was followed by rich and poor, learned and ignorant, old, middle-aged and young[3] of either sex. All conditions were represented, but the monks appear to have come mainly from the middle and lower classes. Anthony's parents were well off; Joseph was a member of an illustrious family and was the chief man of Thmuis;[4] Theodore, the disciple of Pachomius, came from a distinguished home; and one became a monk who was the son of a count, very wealthy and liberally educated;[5] while on the other hand special mention is made of John of Lycopolis as being born of an obscure family, but who was venerated nevertheless by high and low.[6]

Still less is it fair to emphasize their lack of learning, for a diligent study of the Scriptures was universal; books were copied in the cells,[7] and the Pachomian

[1] *H.M.*, prol. 10.   [2] *H.L.*, 18.
[3] Soc., *H E*, iv. 23 ; Soz., *H.E*, vi. 29.
[4] *Coll.*, xvi 1.   [5] *Instit.*, iv. 29.
[6] *Coll*, xxiv. 26.   [7] *Instit*, iv. 12; v. 39

system laid great stress upon educational attainments, providing teaching for those who could not read However, "they neglect many branches of mathematics and the technicalities of dialectics, because they regard such studies as superfluous, and as a useless expenditure of time, seeing that they contribute nothing towards correct living."[1] Joseph was acquainted with Greek thought, and could speak Greek;[2] Theon and three other monks are mentioned as knowing Latin, Greek and Coptic;[3] Paphnutius was very learned in the Old and New Testaments;[4] Evagrius often went to Alexandria and confuted the Greek philosophers;[5] Theodore the Alexandrian reader learned to speak Coptic and acted as interpreter for the great Theodore;[6] Ammon also acquired Coptic;[7] Pachomius had learnt Greek late in life;[8] Piterus was well-informed in many branches of natural philosophy;[9] Eulogius, a monk of Alexandria, was a learned man, having had a good all-round education;[10] Jacob was exceedingly erudite;[11] Simeon of Italy knew no Greek, but was a good Latin scholar;[12] and Nesteros was possessed of great knowledge.[13]

On the other hand, Anthony could only speak Coptic,[14] and the defects in his education resulted from the neglect of his opportunities; and possibly his apparent acquaintance[15] with Greek philosophy was due to the biographer. The Abbot Theodore could speak only a few Greek words, but he was distinguished for his knowledge of the Scriptures, for which, however, he believed that purity of heart, and not a

[1] Soz., H.E., 1. 12.   [2] Coll., xvi. 1.   [3] H.M., 6, 8.
[4] H.L., 47   [5] H.M., 27.   [6] Ep. Ammon., 2, 3.
[7] Ep. Ammon., 9.   [8] Vit. Pash., 60.   [9] Soc , H.E., iv. 23.
[10] H.L., 21   [11] H.L., 47.   [12] Instit., v. 39.
[13] Coll., xiv. 1.   [14] H.L., 21.   [15] Vit., 33, 74, 76.

Social and Intellectual Status

commentary, was necessary.[1] Or knew nothing of letters,[2] and Pambo was an illiterate and had to depend upon another for learning a psalm.[3]

But in the desert they all lived similar lives, endured the same hardships, were occupied in like pursuits, embraced the ascetic ideal of poverty and chastity, and were engaged in the same ceaseless struggle against the principal faults, the eight insidious foes which according to Cassian[4] attacked the monks, of gluttony, fornication, covetousness, anger, dejection, accidie, vainglory, and pride. The only aristocracy which counted was that of spirituality, for the desert ennobled the servants of Christ.[5] So there was a strongly marked individualism: "I have spent forty years in this cell caring for my own salvation," said Pachon of Scete,[6] and that was the typical attitude of early monasticism. Consequently these "athletes" loved to compete with one another in their austerities; and the Nitrian monks are described as "surpassing one another in virtues and being filled with a spirit of rivalry in asceticism, showing forth all virtue, and striving to outdo one another in manner of life."[7] Of Macarius, the Alexandrian, it is said that if he ever heard of anyone having performed a work of asceticism, he was all on fire to do the same,[8] while Palladius[9] describes a meal eaten by Paul the Simple and Anthony, who rivalled one another in austerity. But this characteristic was found in a less degree among the Pachomian monks,[10] and with them rank was reckoned by the length of time they had been in the monastery.

[1] *Instit.*, v. 33 f.
[2] *H.M*, 2.
[3] Soc., *H.E.*, iv. 23.
[4] *Instit.*, v.–xii.; *Coll.*, v.
[5] *Coll*, xxiv. 26.
[6] *H.L.*, 23.
[7] *H.M.*, 23; cf. 8.
[8] *H.L.*, 18.
[9] *H.L.*, 22.
[10] *H.M.*, 3.

3. MONASTICISM AND THE CHURCH

Monasticism was a movement of laymen: neither Anthony nor Pachomius were priests, and so highly did the earliest monks value the desert life of contemplation and the importance of renunciation that they were willing to forego the spiritual help of the Church's Means of Grace. Indeed the hermits can scarcely ever have received Communion, but when the opportunity came, Basil[1] says that Reservation of the Sacrament was practised by the monks of Egypt. Anthony had for many years no opportunity of attending a church or receiving the Communion. But as monastic associations grew up and priests joined, these conditions changed, for churches were established, and the author of *Historia Monachorum* makes frequent references to the Eucharist.[2] But traces of the old attitude are seen in Valens, Hero and Ptolemy,[3] who in their proud self-sufficiency would not receive the Eucharist, and Valens said: " I have no need to become a partaker, for I have seen Christ to-day." There is also mention of a nun, Taor, at Antinoë, who did not go with the others to Communion.[4] Some, however, received the Communion only once a year through excessive reverence, but it was considered best to partake every Sunday.[5] Further, the attitude to the Church is illustrated by Cassian, who includes the desire for the priesthood or diaconate among the temptations of the monk, and repeats an old maxim of the Fathers that was still current: " a monk ought by all means to fly from women and bishops, for neither of them will allow him . . . any longer to care

[1] *Ep.*, 93. [2] 2, 8, 15, 18, 22, 32.
[3] *H.L.*, 25–27. [4] *H.L.*, 59. [5] *Coll.*, xxiii. 21.

Monasticism and the Church

for the quiet of his cell or to continue with pure eyes in divine contemplation through his insight into holy things."[1] Although the attitude of Nathaniel was exceptional, who excused his discourtesy to some bishops by saying : " I am dead both to my lords the bishops and to all the world,"[2] yet we read of Pachomius hiding himself to avoid ordination to the priesthood,[3] of Ammonius on account of the importunities of the people disqualifying himself for the office of a bishop by cutting off his left ear and threatening to slit his tongue,[4] and of Evagrius escaping by flight when Theophilus of Alexandria purposed to make him a bishop.[5] But this attitude was not universal, for Athanasius collected instances in *Ep.* 49 of monks who became bishops.

Notwithstanding, the Church and monasticism were on good terms, and remained in close connection, mainly through the influence of Anthony, Pachomius and Athanasius.

Anthony " observed the rule of the Church most rigidly, and was willing that all the clergy should be honoured above himself. For he was not ashamed to bow his head to bishops and presbyters, and if even a deacon came to him for help he discoursed with him on what was profitable, but gave place to him in prayer, not being ashamed to learn himself."[6] He moreover left his two sheepskins to the bishops Athanasius and Serapion.[7]

Pachomius also was on good terms with the bishops. He had a high appreciation of Athanasius.[8] By the wish of the Bishop of Tentyra, Pachomius built a

---

[1] *Instit*, xi 14, 16, 18 ; *Coll*, 1. 20; iv. 20.   [2] *H L.*, 16.
[3] *Vit. Pach*, 20.   [4] *H L*, 11.   [5] Soc , *H E.*, iv. 23
[6] *Vit Ant*, 67.   [7] *Vit Ant*, 91.   [8] *Ep. Ammon*, 6

church in the village to which the people of the neighbourhood could go on Saturdays and Sundays, and the same bishop wanted Athanasius to ordain him to the priesthood,[1] while the Bishop of Panopolis asked for a monastery near his city.[2] Some bishops, however, did summon Pachomius before them, but it was on account of his visions, not for his monasticism.[3] When clergy visited the Pachomian monasteries their feet were washed by the monks, and clergy who became monks were treated equally with laymen in the matter of the rules, but reverence was paid to their office.[4]

Of Schenoudi it may be briefly said that he was, unlike the other great monastic figures in Egypt, a priest,[5] and that he is represented as being on good terms with the Church.[6]

Athanasius was deeply interested in monasticism. Although moderation marked his references to marriage,[7] yet throughout his life he held virginity in the highest estimation. This is seen at an early period in the *De Incarnatione*.[8] Later[9] he wrote as follows: "There are two ways in life as touching these matters. The one, the more moderate and ordinary, I mean marriage; the other, angelic and unsurpassed, namely virginity. Now if a man choose the way of the world, namely marriage, he is not indeed to blame, yet he will not receive such great gifts as the other. For he will receive, since he too brings forth fruit, namely thirtyfold. But if a man embrace the holy and unearthly way, even though as compared with the former it be rugged and hard to accomplish, yet it has the more wonderful gifts, for it grows the perfect fruit,

---

[1] *Vit. Pach.*, 20. [2] *Vit. Pach.*, 51. [3] *Vit Pach.*, 72.
[4] *Vit. Pach.*, 18. [5] *M.*, 1. [6] *M*, 67 ff.
[7] *Fest. epp*, 1. 3; x 4. [8] 27, 48, 51. [9] *c.* 350–3.

namely an hundredfold."[1] Not long afterwards (354 A.D.) he said: "Is it not a great wonder to make a damsel live as a virgin and a young man live in continence and an idolater come to know Christ?"[2] Also, in his *Apologia ad Constant.* (33), he wrote: "The Son of God ... in addition to all His other benefits bestowed this also upon us that we should possess upon earth in the state of virginity a picture of the holiness of angels. Accordingly such as have attained this virtue, the Catholic Church has been accustomed to call the brides of Christ, and the heathen who see this express their admiration of them as the temples of the Word. For indeed this holy and heavenly profession is nowhere established, but only among us Christians, and it is a very strong argument that with us is to be found the genuine and true religion." And once more in the *Historia Arianorum* (25) he said: "How many unmarried women who were before ready to enter upon marriage now remained virgins to Christ! How many young men, seeing the examples of others, embraced the monastic life! How many fathers persuaded their children, and how many were urged by their children not to be hindered from Christian asceticism!"

Again, it is possible that Athanasius was at an early period in his life a disciple of Anthony.[3] However, at the time of his election to the episcopate he was himself called "an ascetic,"[4] and Gregory Nazianzen[5] eulogised his austerities as follows: "Let one praise him in his fastings and prayers as if he had been disembodied and immaterial." He commended monasticism in church, and his words led Ammon to

---

[1] *ad Amun.*   [2] *ad Dracont.*, 7.   [3] *Vit. Ant.*, prol.
[4] *Apol. c. Arian.*, 6.   [5] *Or.*, xxi. 10.

become a monk;[1] it was through him that the monastic life became known at Rome;[2] his name was associated with the authorship of Anthony's biography;[3] and Cassian states that the festal letters of the Bishop of Alexandria were sent to the monasteries.[4] In 330 he visited Tabennesis, when Pachomius and his monks went out with singing and thanksgiving to meet him,[5] and in 363 he made a detailed visitation of the Pachomian monasteries, seeing the cells, refectories, places of prayer, etc., and was enthusiastic.[6] Indeed he loved the Tabennesiot monks,[7] and when they came to Alexandria they were received with much kindness by him.[8] On the death of Theodore he was greatly grieved, and wrote a letter of consolation to Orsisius.[9]

It is no wonder, therefore, that Athanasius exercised a great, powerful and restraining influence over the Egyptian monks, to which enthusiastic testimony was borne by Gregory Nazianzen: " Let hermits celebrate him who lent wings to their course, cenobites their lawgiver ";[10] and again, " during his intercourse with them the great Athanasius, who was always the mediator and reconciler of all other men, like Him Who made peace through His Blood between things which were at variance, reconciled the solitary with the community life. . . . Thus he combined the two, and so united the partisans of both calm action and active calm as to convince them that the monastic life is characterised by steadfastness of disposition rather than by bodily retirement. . . . Whatever he thought was a law for them, whatever on the contrary

[1] *ep. Ammon.*, 1.   [2] Jer., *ep*, 127.   [3] Greg. Naz., *Or.*, xxi. 5.
[4] *Coll.*, x. 2.   [5] *Vit. Pach.*, 20.   [6] *Vit. Pach*, 92.
[7] *Vit. Pach.*, 88   [8] *Vit Pach*, 77
[9] *Vit. Pach.*, 96. Athan., *ep.*, 58   [10] *Or*, xxi 10.

Monasticism and the Church

he disapproved they abjured. His decisions were to them the tables of Moses, and they paid him more reverence than is due from men to the saints."[1] In consequence, therefore, of the alliance between Athanasius and the monks, he had their devotion and support when in his person orthodoxy was challenged by the Arians and the Egyptian Church became a persecuted body; indeed, in 356 he found refuge among the monks.[2] Anthony showed the strongest aversion not only to Arians, but also to the Meletians, and reiterated his warnings as he bid his monks farewell before his death.[3] Pachomius had a like antipathy to the Arians;[4] another monk expressed a similar attitude to Manichæans;[5] and it is significant that the monastery of Pabau was searched for Athanasius when he was in hiding.[6]

But it is of interest to notice that there were Meletian monks before the Council of Tyre (335), for mention is made of such a monastery at Ptemencyrcis, where Arsenius, whom Athanasius was accused of murdering, lay concealed.[7]

One other factor tended to preserve monasticism from drifting away in antagonism to the Church; that was the importance attached by the monks to obedience,[8] although there is an indication in the letter of Athanasius to Dracontius[9] that the different ideals prevented the relations from always being smooth.

Unfortunately, however, at the close of the century the attitude of the monks towards the Bishop of

[1] *Or.*, xxi. 19 f.
[2] Greg Naz., *Or*, xxi. 19.
[3] *Vit. Ant.*, 68 ff., 89, 91.
[4] *Ep Ammon.*, 6, cf. 22.
[5] *H M.*, 11.
[6] *Vit. Pach.*, 88
[7] *Athan., Apol. c. Arian.*, 67.
[8] e.g. *Instit.*, IV. 26.
[9] *Ep.*, xlix. 8, 9.

Alexandria became embittered, for although Theophilus was so interested in monasticism as to ask Ammon for an account of his experiences at Pabau,[1] he caused great anger and indignation among the monks generally by his condemnation of the Anthropomorphites.[2]

4. Peaceful Simplicity of the Monastic Life and its Interruptions

The monks lived a quiet, simple existence for spiritual purposes,[3] away from the distractions of town life. There in solitude, going gradually further away from human habitations, they ate the plainest food, slept little and were engaged in manual labour to supply the simplest necessaries of existence. Usually it was the sedentary occupation of twisting leaves of palm trees into mats and baskets, though the Pachomian monks were employed in various trades. The importance and value of work was recognised not only by Pachomius but by Anthony, in precept and example, Abraham, who discoursed on the harm of idleness,[4] and the Egyptian monks generally.[5] It was regarded as an anchor, which kept the heart in the perfectly secure harbour of the cell.[6] But the place of work in the life of the monks did not assume quite the same importance in Lower Egypt[7] as it did in the highly organised industrial communities of Pachomius; and Abraham believed that the monk's work in the open air tended to "scatter to the winds all his concentra-

---

[1] *Ep Ammon.* [2] *Coll.*, x 2; Soz., *H.E.*, viii. 11 f.
[3] *Coll.*, iii. 1; xix. 2, 5, 6, 8; *Instit*, viii 18.
[4] *Coll.*, xxiv. 12. [5] *Instit.*, ii. 14; x. 22; Jer., *Ep.*, 125.
[6] *Instit*, ii. 14. [7] The references to work in *H.M.* are few.

Simplicity of Monastic Life

tion of mind and all the keenness of his vision of aim."[1]

A pleasing feature of the monks was the charitable work which they were able to do by the proceeds of their labour. Palæmon and his disciple Pachomius gave to the poor;[2] the Pachomian monks provided for those in prison;[3] and Schenoudi did much for those in want.[4] Serapion in the region of Arsinoitis distributed food to the needy, and boats full of food and clothing used to be sent to the poor of Alexandria;[5] Apollo relieved large numbers in time of famine;[6] Pæsius and Isaias, sons of a merchant, on receiving their inheritance occupied themselves with work among the poor;[7] relief was given to poor monasteries;[8] and Cassian says that the monks not only relieve pilgrims and visitors but "actually collect an enormous store of provisions and food, and distribute it in the parts of Libya, which suffer from famine and barrenness, and also in the cities, to those who are pining away in the squalor of prison."[9] Moreover, cures were frequently effected through the agency of the monks, but the latter were not always well received by the pagans when they entered the villages.[10]

Many were reported to have lived to a great age; probably, however, this was exaggerated, for there was very little to mark the passage of time in their uneventful lives. No doubt they suffered considerably from fevers and eye troubles, but little is heard of their ailments.

Love of nature was slightly known, but here and there we have appreciations of the attractions of the

[1] *Coll.*, xxiv. 3.   [2] *Vit Pach*, 4.   [3] *H L*, 32.
[4] *Zoega*, 212.   [5] *H M.*, 20.   [6] *H.M.*, 8.
[7] *H L*, 14.   [8] *H.L.*, 10
[9] *Instit*, x 22; cf. *Coll*, xiv 4   [10] *Coll*, xv. 5.

desert. They admired the beauty and simplicity of nature;[1] and when Anthony was questioned on the deprivation of the comfort of books, he made reply: "My book is the nature of things that are made, and it is present whenever I wish to read the words of God."[2] John complained that there were too many in the desert, and compared it with the former days when "a greater freedom was afforded to us in a wide expanse of the wilderness," where " in the seclusion of larger retreats we are caught up to those celestial ecstasies ": he went on also to say, " I frequented with insatiable desire and all my heart the peaceful retreats of the desert and that life which can only be compared to the bliss of the angels "; and he complained that the large number of people was " cramping the freedom of the desert wilderness."[3] No sayings in Egypt, however, reached the panegyric of Jerome, "O Desert, bright with the flowers of Christ! O Solitude, whence come the stones of which, in the Apocalypse, the city of the Great King is built! O Wilderness, gladdened with God's especial presence! What keeps you in the world, my brother, you who are above the world? How long shall gloomy roofs oppress you? How long shall smoky cities immure you?"[4] "Oh, that I could behold the desert, lovelier to me than any city."[5]

But on the other hand, Cassian wrote of "the wretched desert,"[6] and Abbot Abraham saw little attraction in it, which consisted of "sandy wastes horrid with the barrenness of nature and districts overwhelmed by living incrustations";[7] the monk

---

[1] Soz., *H.E.*, i. 12.   [2] Soc., *H.E.*, iv. 23.   [3] *Coll.*, xix. 5.
[4] Jer., *Ep*, xiv. 10.   [5] Jer., *Ep*, 2.   [6] *Instit.*, iv. 25.
[7] *Coll.*, xxiv. 12.

Simplicity of Monastic Life

ought to avoid pleasant recesses where there are plenty of fruit and pleasant gardens and fertile ground, for the mind is disturbed by the necessity of cultivating good soil; therefore " we delight only in this squalor and prefer to all luxuries this dreadful and vast desert, and cannot compare any riches of a fertile soil to these barren sands."[1]

Another characteristic of the records of the Egyptian monks is the number of animal stories which centre round them, and these, notwithstanding their absurdities, testify to the affection with which the wild animals of the desert were regarded, in spite of the danger to life from hyenas, etc.[2] Interest was shown in the habits of birds, beasts and serpents.[3] Macarius the Alexandrian is said to have obtained milk from a buffalo who followed him through the desert to his cell, and to have cured a young hyena of blindness.[4] Anthony was visited by two lions as he was burying Paul, which licked his hands and feet, and, pawing the ground, digged a hole large enough for the body.[5] Theon used to mingle with the animals of the desert and to give them drink, and tracks of buffaloes, wild asses and gazelles were found near his abode.[6] In the Dialogue of Sulpitius we read of the old monk who fed a lion with dates,[7] of a she-wolf who regularly appeared at dinner-time to share a monk's meal,[8] of the lioness who led a monk to her den in order to cure her whelp of blindness and who in gratitude presented him with a skin which he used as a cloak,[9] and of the ibex who taught a monk what plants to eat and what to avoid.[10]

Indeed no small part of the monastic records is

---

[1] *Coll.*, xxiv. 2. [2] *H L.*, 16, 23. [3] *Coll.*, xvi. 2.
[4] *H L.*, 18.   [5] Jer., *Vit. Paul*, 16. [6] *H M.*, 6.
[7] i. 13. [8] i. 14. [9] i. 15. [10] i. 16.

devoted to the supernatural and miraculous in which the Coptic mind revelled. Palladius is said to have recounted as many as seventy wonders, the *Vita Antonii* is full of conflicts with demons, and miraculous events are frequent in the records of Pachomius and Schenoudi. Some allowance, however, must be made for exaggeration, as the stories passed from one to another, and " we must in justice take into our account the powers which certainly accrue to mind and will when they are purified and strengthened. Insight into character, that strange yet real power called ' second sight,' healthful influence upon the mental and physical state of others, the gift of attracting and controlling the wildest creatures of the desert are endowments which we should expect and which we find among the best of the solitaries."[1] However, by the end of the fourth century the belief in the power of demons had become somewhat modified, and Serenus was not sure whether it was due to the power of the Cross which had beaten back the malice of the demons or to the relaxed efforts of those evil spirits who did not consider that the later monks were worthy of the fierce onslaughts with which the earlier anchorites had been attacked.[2]

The quiet monotony of their lives was relieved occasionally by the visits of pilgrims, to which reference will be made later ; but less welcome were the curious sightseers who came without any serious intention of studying the monastic life.[3] They were annoyed too by thieves,[4] and were liable to be seized for military service,[5] while in an invasion of barbarians a monk

[1] E. W Watson, *Church Quarterly Review*, April, 1907, p. 123.
[2] *Coll.*, vii. 23.   [3] *Coll*, xviii 2.
[4] *H M*, 9   [5] *H M*, 8.

was even taken captive.¹ The monks, moreover, from time to time were involved in the serious disturbances of the time. In the Arian troubles they frequently suffered; at the time of Gregory's arrival in Alexandria the virgins and monks were ill-treated,² as well as later when the monasteries were overthrown.³ Anthony emerged from his retirement and appeared in Alexandria to support the cause of Athanasius. When the latter died, the Nitrian monks joined in the opposition to an Arian successor, but their enemies " assailed and disturbed and terribly harassed the monastic institutions in the desert, and armed men rushed in the most ferocious manner upon those who were utterly defenceless and who would not lift an arm to repel their violence, so that numbers of unresisting victims were in this manner slaughtered with a degree of wanton cruelty beyond description."⁴ Some were deported to an island in one of the lakes, others to Palestine, accompanied by Melania who ministered to their needs.⁵ The Origenistic controversy at the end of the century also affected the monks in Nitria, for the Origenists were expelled (*c.* 400) from their monasteries by Theophilus, Bishop of Alexandria.⁶

¹ *Vit. Pach.*, 54.
² Athan, *Epist. Encyl.*, 3 and 4; *Apol c. Arian.*, 30.
³ Ath., *Hist. Arian.*, 72.   ⁴ Soc., *H.E*, iv. 22.
⁵ Soc., *H.E.*, iv. 24; *H.L.*, 46.   ⁶ Jer, *Epp.*, 87, 89, 90, 92.

V

THE SPREAD OF EGYPTIAN MONASTICISM

THERE were certain factors which contributed to the spread of monasticism in Egypt and in other countries, apart from the causes which led to its rise. In the first place, its novelty no doubt to some extent fanned the enthusiasm with which this new mode of life was eagerly adopted by Christians of the fourth century. The personality and fame of the great figures of monasticism also furthered the cause, for we are told that the example of celebrated monks brought the call to some;[1] and in this connection the visits of Anthony to Alexandria were of extraordinary interest to the people of that city, who had the opportunity of seeing so remarkable a figure of the age.

The *Vita Antonii* must have exercised a great influence and caused many another besides Augustine[2] to embark on a life of renunciation. It was written during the lifetime of Athanasius (*d.* 373), who was probably its author, and it was translated into Latin by Evagrius (*c.* 373). With regard to the influence of another monastic biography, the *Vita Martini*, the following testimony occurs in Sulpit., *Dial.*, i. 23: in Alexandria " it is almost better known to all than it is to yourself. It has passed through Egypt, Nitria, the Thebaid, and the whole of the regions of Memphis.

---

[1] *Coll.*, iii. 4.   [2] *Confess.*, VIII.

I found it being read by a certain old man in the desert."

Again, what must have appealed to large numbers was that the monastic life could be followed by all of any rank in society. Poverty or riches, learning or ignorance, age or sex formed no impediment. And then there was, as it has been seen, the enthusiastic approval and support of the great Athanasius.

Further, the story of Egyptian monasticism was brought to other countries by the work of Athanasius, and by the pilgrimages to Egyptian deserts, which men and women made, throughout the century, to study at first hand monasticism in the land which saw its rise. This resulted in the detailed and widespread knowledge of the life led by the Egyptian monks.

1. PILGRIMAGES TO EGYPT

Hilarion, the originator of monasticism in Palestine,[1] derived his enthusiasm from Egypt. He was born (c. 291), near Gaza, of pagan parents, who sent their son, on account of his abilities, to be educated in Alexandria. There he became a Christian, and taking no pleasure in worldly amusements, but fired with the desire to see Anthony, he set off to visit the great hermit. After staying two months with him, he could endure no longer the crowds that visited Anthony, returned home and pursued the ascetic life of an Egyptian monk, wearing the coat of skin that had been given to him by Anthony himself. So great became his fame that people flocked to him and many adopted his mode of life, " for as yet there were no

[1] Of whom Jerome wrote a semi-historical life in c 390, cf. Soz., H.E., iii. 14.

monasteries in Palestine, nor had anyone known a monk in Syria before the saintly Hilarion. It was he who originated this mode of life and devotion, and who first trained men to it in that province. The Lord Jesus had in Egypt the aged Anthony: in Palestine He had the youthful Hilarion."[1] Later in his life he visited the place where Anthony had died, and had the happiness of reclining on the saint's bed, of seeing his garden, and perhaps his burial-place.[2]

Epiphanius, who had visited Egypt, established himself not far away, near Besanduc; and he " became most celebrated in Egypt and Palestine by his attainments in monastic philosophy," and was chosen afterwards Bishop of Salamis in Cyprus.[3]

Eustathius. Monasticism was originally introduced into the districts of Pontus and Cappadocia by Eustathius, who was born *c.* 300, and was the son of Eulalius, Bishop of Sebaste.[4] Eustathius was educated in Egypt under Arius;[5] and on his return he enthusiastically adopted an ascetic mode of life, and gained many disciples. Sozomen[6] states that he " founded a society of monks in Armenia, Paphlagonia and Pontus, and became the author of a zealous discipline, both as to what meats were to be partaken of or to be avoided, what garments were to be worn, and what customs and exact course of conduct were to be adopted," and the same writer[7] calls him " a leader of the best monks." Further, he exercised considerable influence upon Basil, for when the latter returned from his travels, he found the disciples of Eustathius leading ascetic lives, wherein he says : " I felt that I had found a help

---

[1] *Vit. Hil.*, 14. [2] *Vit Hil.*, 31. [3] Soz, *H.E.*, vi. 32.
[4] Soc, *H.E.*, ii. 43 [5] Basil, *Ep*, 263. [6] *H.E.*, iii. 14.
[7] *H.E.*, viii 27.

to my own salvation "; and Eustathius paid frequent visits to Basil's monastery on the Isis, and to his home at Annesi, " living as friend with friend and discoursing together day and night."[1] Indeed, Sozomen[2] stated, " some assert that he was the author of the ascetic books commonly attributed to Basil of Cappadocia "; but to what extent Basil's works are Eustathian there is no evidence to show. The two main points to be drawn from Eustathius's career are the Egyptian origin of his monasticism, and his influence over Basil.

Basil, the Great, was born at Cæsarea (*c.* 329) of a distinguished family in Cappadocia ; and his father and mother were devoted Christians.[3] He received his early religious instruction from his grandmother Macrina, who had come under the influence of Origenistic teaching through the writings of Gregory Thaumaturgus.[4] Various members of his family began to devote themselves to an ascetic life through the influence of his sister Macrina, who had laid upon herself the vow of virginity.[5] After a liberal education under the most renowned teachers of the time Basil returned to Cæsarea, in 356, and largely through the advice of his sister he determined to adopt the ascetic life. For the purpose of studying asceticism at first hand, he started on his travels after being baptized and ordained reader, and visited Egypt, Palestine and Mesopotamia. Basil has left an account in Epistle 223 of his feelings at this period in the following words : " I wept many tears over my miserable life, and I prayed that guidance might be vouchsafed me to admit me to the doctrines of true religion. First of all was I minded to make some mending of my ways, long

[1] *Ep.,* 223.   [2] *H E.,* III 14.   [3] Greg. Naz., *Or.,* 43.
[4] *Ep.,* 204.   [5] Greg. Naz., *Vit. Macr.*

perverted as they were by my intimacy with wicked men. Then I read the Gospel, and I saw there that a great means of reaching perfection was the selling of one's goods, the sharing them with the poor, the giving up of all care for this life, and the refusal to allow the soul to be turned by any sympathy to things of earth. And I prayed that I might find some one of the brethren who had chosen this way of life, that with him I might cross life's short and troubled strait. And many did I find in Alexandria, and many in the rest of Egypt, and others in Palestine, and in Coele-Syria, and in Mesopotamia. I admired their continence in living, and their endurance in toil; I was amazed at their persistence in prayer, and at their triumphing over sleep; subdued by no natural necessity, ever keeping their soul's purpose high and free, in hunger, in thirst, in cold, in nakedness, they never yielded to the body; they were never willing to waste attention on it; always, as though living in a flesh that was not theirs, they showed in very deed what it is to sojourn for a while in this life, and what to have one's citizenship and home in heaven. All this moved my admiration. I called these men's lives blessed, in that they did in deed show that they "bear about in their body the dying of Jesus." And I prayed that I, too, as far as in me lay, might imitate them." In 358 Basil returned and started on his monastic career that was to become so famous. The Egyptian origin of his system and his debt to Pachomius are manifest; like him, he founded cenobia, laid stress on manual labour, and advocated a moderate asceticism. Moreover, Basil exercised an enduring influence on later developments. In the East, the later monks held in venera-

Pilgrimages to Egypt

tion the Basilian Rules as the oldest collection of monastic regulations, but the general tendency of Eastern monasticism was to regard the solitary as superior to the cenobitic life. In the West, however, Basil's influence was more marked. His Rules were translated into Latin by Rufinus at the close of the fourth century, and his ideals formed a factor in the eclectic monasticism of Italy. But the main direction of Basil's influence was to be seen in the great work accomplished for monasticism by Benedict, who owed much to the great Cappadocian.

Melania. In 373 a great Roman lady, named Melania, spent six months in Egypt. She provided Palladius with information on various events in Nitria before his arrival,[1] received presents from Pambo of Nitria and Macarius the Alexandrian,[2] and in 374 accompanied and ministered to the Egyptian bishops and others who were banished to Palestine.[3] She then settled in Jerusalem, where she had a convent of fifty virgins; and in close association lived Rufinus with a similar establishment for men, where they received visitors for many years [4]

Jerome and Paula Before Paula, the wealthy Roman widow of noble birth, settled in 386 at Bethlehem with her daughter Eustochium and Jerome, they made a pilgrimage to Egypt, of which Jerome wrote an account in his *Epistle* 108 : " No sooner did Paula come in sight of it (Nitria) than there came to meet her the reverend and estimable bishop, the confessor Isidore, accompanied by countless multitudes of monks, many of whom were of priestly or of Levitical rank. On seeing these, Paula rejoiced to behold the

---

[1] *H L*, 5, 9, 10, 18.   [2] *H L.*, 10, 18
[3] *H L.*, 46 ; Paul. of Nola, *Ep.*, 29.   [4] *H.L.*, 46.

Lord's glory manifested in them, but protested that she had no claim to be received with such honour. Need I speak of the Macarii, Arsenius, Serapion, or other pillars of Christ! Was there any cell that she did not enter! Or any man at whose feet she did not throw herself! In each of His saints she believed that she saw Christ Himself; and whatever she bestowed upon them she rejoiced to feel that she had bestowed it upon the Lord. Her enthusiasm was wonderful, and her endurance scarcely credible in a woman. Forgetful of her sex and of her weakness she even desired to make her abode, together with the girls who accompanied her, among these thousands of monks. And as they were all willing to welcome her, she might perhaps have sought and obtained permission to do so, had she not been drawn away by a still greater passion for the holy places." At Bethlehem they established a monastery for men, three convents for women, and a hospice for strangers.[1]

Other pilgrims included the author of the *Peregrinatio Silviæ*, who was very probably a Spanish virgin, named Etheria (or Eucheria), and belonged to a Galician convent, for which she wrote the account of her many travels;[2] Rufinus,[3] Silvania, the sister-in-law of Rufinus, who travelled with Palladius to Egypt on his first or second journey,[4] Photinus, a learned deacon from Cappadocia,[5] and the anti-Origenist monk, Theodore, who visited the monasteries of Nitria.[6]

Literary Pilgrims. Of great importance were the visits of those whose accounts are preserved :

(*a*) Palladius, a Galatian, who in *c.* 386 became a

[1] *Epp.*, 108, 66.
[2] M. Férotin, *Revue des questions historiques*, 1903, pp. 367 ff.
[3] Jer., *Ep.*, 3.   [4] *H L.*, 55.   [5] *Coll*, x 3.
[6] Jer., *Ep.*, 89.

Work of Athanasius

monk on the Mount of Olives, spent the years 388 to 399 and 406 to 412 in Egypt. The latter period was passed in Upper Egypt, while the former was devoted to a stay of two or three years in the neighbourhood of Alexandria, of one year at Nitria, and of nine years in the cells.[1] About the year 420 he wrote the famous account of his experiences in the *Historia Lausiaca*, so-called from its dedication to Lausus, chamberlain of Theodosius II.

(*b*) A party of seven travellers started from the monastery on the Mount of Olives and spent the winter of 394–5 in Egypt. The record of their journey is given in the *Historia Monachorum in Ægypto*, which was translated into Latin by Rufinus.

(*c*) Cassian was in Egypt between the years 390 and 400; and his visit embraced the Delta, Nitria, and Scete, but he did not proceed to the Thebaid. Consequently his account in *Instit*, iv. 1–18, which deals mainly with the Pachomian system, is not of great importance. His *Institutes* and *Collations* were published 420–430.

(*d*) Postumian (*c*. 402) visited Alexandria and the Thebaid, and his experiences, full of marvellous events, are described in the first dialogue of his friend Sulpitius.

2. THE WORK OF ATHANASIUS

Although there were ascetics living alone and apparently in associations at an earlier date in Italy,[2] it was not until the visit of Athanasius in 340 that monasticism in that country received a great inspiration. He was accompanied by the monks Isidore and

---

[1] *H L*, 7, 18
[2] *Acta Sanctorum*, Mau, t iii., p. 283; *Ital. Sacr.*, 1. 405, 657; iii. 527; iv. 40.

Ammonius the Tall,[1] and remained in Rome and various Italian towns until 346, so that there was ample time for him to inspire the people with the example of Egyptian monasticism. The noble Roman lady, Marcella, was greatly influenced by him, from whom she " heard of the life of the blessed Anthony, then still alive, and of the monasteries in the Thebaid founded by Pachomius, and of the discipline laid down for virgins and for widows ";[2] she then began to lead an ascetic life in monastic seclusion at her home on the Aventine.[3] She was a friend of the famous Paula, and was responsible for her conversion to the same mode of life.[4] The ground had thus been prepared by Athanasius for the great impetus given to the ascetic movement by Jerome during his stay in Rome (382–385 A.D), and Epiphanius, Bishop of Salamis.[5]

Moreover, it appears that the influence of Athanasius is to be found in the monasticism of Eusebius of Vercelli, and Martin of Tours, as well as Augustine.

In Northern Italy, Eusebius, who became Bishop of Vercelli (c. 340), founded a monastery for his clergy. It is true that he was exiled to Egypt from 355 to 363, but he probably received his desire for a monastic life from Athanasius, when he was living at Rome.[6] For it would seem that the foundation of the institution of Eusebius at Vercelli cannot probably be postponed to his return from exile, for Ambrose[7] said that although his fellow-exile, Dionysius, Bishop of Milan, died from his hardships, Eusebius survived on account of his power of endurance, which had been won by a long monastic life ; moreover, when he was exiled in 352

[1] H.L , 1 ; Soc , H E., iv 23
[2] Jer , Ep., cxxvii. 5.
[3] Jer , Ep , xlvii. 3.
[4] Jer., Ep., xlvi 1.
[5] Soz., H E , vi 32
[6] Ital. Sacr , iv 753.
[7] Ep., lxiii. 70 f.

to a place beyond the Po, a few miles from Vercelli, he took with him his disciples.[1]

The great figure of the earliest monasticism in Gaul was Martin. He was born (c. 336) of pagan parents, who were " of no mean rank." From his earliest years at Pavia, in Italy, his mind was set on the service of God; and when he was twelve years old, he would have liked, had his age allowed, to have become a hermit, " his mind being always engaged on matters pertaining to the monasteries and to the Church."[2] It is not, however, stated in what way he became attracted to the monastic life. But it is very probable that his inspiration came from the knowledge and practice of Egyptian monasticism in Italy which had been spread by Athanasius and Eusebius. This is confirmed by the general character of the system he established at Marmoutiers (c. 372), which appears to have been based on the Antonian type of an association of eremites. It was, however, more of a common life than at Nitria, but it fell short of being a cenobitic community. His eighty followers lived in mountain caves; all things were possessed in common; they took their food together; " most of them were clothed in garments of camels' hair; any dress approaching to softness was there deemed criminal, and this must be thought the more remarkable, because many among them were such as were deemed of noble rank " ; and " no art was practised there, except that of transcribers, and even this was assigned to the brethren of younger years, while the elders spent their time in prayer. Rarely did any one of them go beyond the cell, except when they assembled at the place of prayer."[3]

In the last few years of the fourth century monas-

[1] *Ital Sacr.*, iv. 754.   [2] *Vit. Martin*, 2.   [3] *Vit.*, 10

150 Christian Monasticism in Egypt

ticism was introduced to Africa by the great Augustine, who in his *Confessions* (viii. 6) related the surprising fact that he had not even heard of Anthony and Egyptian monasticism; but in a conversation the African Christian, Pontitianus, told him of the great monk and of the deep impression which the *Vita Antonii* had made upon himself and a friend, when they came upon a certain cottage during a walk where they found the book. Shortly afterwards, when Augustine heard the voice bidding him "take up and read," and the great light came upon him, his mind was still occupied with St. Anthony.[1] His baptism followed in 387, and having spent some time at Rome, where he had the opportunity of seeing the lives led by the monks,[2] he returned to Africa and embraced the monastic life, which found speedily many imitators under his fostering care.

Further, there are two persons enveloped in some obscurity—Mar Awgin of Clysma, and Marcus of Memphis.

Mar Awgin, or *Eugenius*, is traditionally regarded as the introducer of monasticism into Mesopotamia. He is said to have been a pearl-fisher at Clysma, near Suez, and to have become a disciple of Pachomius before the year 330. The story continues that he then departed to Mesopotamia, built a monastery in the mountains near Nisibis before 333, or (according to Assemani, *Bibl. Orient. III*, ii. 14) before 325, and died in old age in 363. But J. Labourt[3] has shown that the life of Mar Awgin[4] cannot be regarded as

[1] *Confessions*, viii 12   [2] *de mor. eccl.*, 70.
[3] *Le Christianisme dans l'Empire Perse*, pp 302 ff.
[4] P. Bedjan, *Acta Martyrum et Sanctorum*, iii., pp. 376 ff.

historical, and that any facts underlying it belong to a much later date.

Marcus of Memphis. Little is known of the early monastic tendencies in Spain, but the chief interest of this period from the ascetic point of view lies in the Priscillianist movement, which arose *c.* 375.[1] It was a mysterious sect ; its doings were surrounded with secrecy, but its general character was a marked asceticism. Communities came to be established, to which admission was gained after a time of probation ; they renounced their property and lived a common life.[2] Its inspiration came from a certain Marcus of Memphis, who went from Egypt to Spain.

[1] Sulpit., *Hist. Sacr* , ii. 46 ff.
[2] H. Leclerq, *Dict d'Arch Chrét* , t. II, pt. 2, p 3220 f.

CONCLUSION

EGYPTIAN monasticism represents in the main two tendencies—one to the solitary, the other to the cenobitic life, and between the two is the association of eremites. The writers of the period were very divided as to the relative merits of the solitary and the cenobitic life; Cassian [1] and Sozomen [2] regarded the solitary life as the pinnacle of excellence, while Basil,[3] Gregory Naz.,[4] Jerome,[5] and Augustine,[6] preferred cenobitism. For a time Antonian monasticism was the more popular and prevailed in the East; but it was the cenobitism of Pachomius that has had the most influence on later developments, and thereon were founded the systems of Basil and Benedict. No doubt H. B. Workman[7] is correct in saying: "If, instead of devoting his pen to the praise of the hermit life, Athanasius had written an account of the community life inaugurated by Pachomius and established by him under a Rule, the two centuries that were to elapse before its principles were developed by St. Benedict might have been considerably shortened. As it was, Pachomius suffered the neglect which too often attends those who are before their age, nor were his monasteries free from the defects of first attempts." So, while Anthony was the great inspirer

---

[1] *Coll., Præf.*   [2] *H.E*, vi. 31.
[3] *Regulæ Fusius Tractatæ*, 7.   [4] *Orat*, 21.   [5] *Ep.*, 125.
[6] *de mor. eccl.*, 31.   [7] *Evolution of the Monastic Ideal*, p. 89.

of the rise of monasticism, and his romantic figure was regarded with love and reverence by his own and succeeding ages, it was to Pachomius, the organizer, that the West owes its great debt for the form of monasticism that has exercised so profound an influence upon the history of the Church and of civilization.

The Rise of Christian monasticism in Egypt has now been traced to the close of the fourth century; and in that early stage of development it left its mark upon the age. On the one hand, the monastic movement gained for celibacy an excessive importance in contemporary Christian thought, and brought about a certain indifference to the claims of the State and family life; it exaggerated the spiritual value of environment, and it tended to lower the standard of ordinary Christian conduct by the establishment of a higher morality for the more earnest. But at the same time it taught a higher regard for manual work and education, the importance of Bible study, the spiritual equality of rich and poor, the value of solitude and contemplation, and the need of discipline in the Christian life; it was the school of saints; it offered a great protest against materialism; it emphasized the need of ethical preparation for the Future Life; and it left an imperishable example of self-denial to all followers of Him, Who cried: "If any man will come after Me, let him deny himself, and take up his cross and follow Me."

INDEX

Abraham, 52 f, 134-6
Accidie, 83, 127
Achilleus, 63
Achoris, 88
Admission, 100 f, 112, 115, 122, 151
Aesculapius, 19
Africa, 50
African Monasticism, 149 f.
Ages of monks, 135
Akhmim, 93
Alexandria, 16 f, 25 f, 27-30, 33 f, 36-40, 43, 45 f, 48 f, 51, 63, 73, 81, 83, 88, 96, 104, 126, 132, 135, 139 f, 141, 144, 147
Amatalis, 120
Amatas, 68, 80
Ambrose, 148
Amélineau, E, 109
Ammon, 36, 109, 126, 131 f, 134
Ammonas, 80
Ammonius Saccas, 27 f, 43
Ammonius the Tall, 83, 121, 129, 148
Amoun, 81 f, 84
Animal food, 14, 16, 30-2, 45, 47, 106, cp. 27 f.
— stories, 137
Annesi, 143
Anthony, S, 52, 56, 58 f, 68-75, 77-80, 82, 84, 86, 110, 125-9, 131-4, 136 f., 139-42, 148, 150, 152 f.
Anthropomorphites, 134
Antinoé, 77, 120, 128
Antonii, Vita, 70-4, 79, 138, 140, 150
Antoninus Pius, 66
Aotas, 91
Apelles, 88

Aphraates, 50
Apis, 19, 28
Apollo, 113 f, 135
Apollonius of Memphis, 19
Apollonius of Monchosis, 94
Apollonius of Nitria, 82 f
Apollonius of Tyana, 16, 27, 31
Apollophanes, 43
Apollos, 122
Apophthegmata, 74
Apphianus, 50
Apuleius, 32, 54
Archebius, 78, 123
Arians, 62, 64, 73, 133, 139
Arius, 142
Arius, Bishop of Panopolis, 93
Armenia, 142
Arsenius, 133
Arsenius of Nitria, 146
Arsinoite district, 60, 88, 135
Arsisius, 110
Ascetic rivalry, 127
Asceticism, Asiatic, 26, 49, 51
— Christian, 38-53, 69
— Egyptian, 20, 28-32, 38, 51
— Greek, 17 f, 26-8, 38, 51
— Indian, 14-16
— Jewish, 22-4, 32-5, 38, 51
Asoka, 15
Assemani, J. S., 150
Associations of eremites, 78-90, 149, 152
Athanasius, 64, 73, 92, 110, 129-133, 139-141, 147-50, 152
Athenagoras, 49
Athens, 49
Athribe, 120
Atripe, 111
Augustine, 140, 148, 150, 152
Ausonius, 109
Austerities, 105, 108, 121 f.

154

Index

Babylon, 88
Basil, 128, 142–5, 152
Basilian rules, 145
Basilides, 36, 46
Bechre, 119
Bedjan, P, 150
Benedict, 145, 152
Besanduc, 142
Bethlehem, 145 f
Bgoul, 111 f.
Blemmyes, 63
B'nai Q'yama, 50 f
Body, the, 27 f, 31, 33 f, 39–41, 48, 58, 62, 144
Book of the Dead, 30, 58
British School of Archæology, 15
Buddhism, 14–17, 22
Budge, E A W, 31, 123
Burkitt, F C, 51
Busiris Tripolitana, 73
Butler, C., 18, 68, 70, 74, 81

Cæsarea, 143
Calamus, desert of, 78
Canopus, 96
Cappadocia, 26, 142 f, 146
Caracalla, 63
Carpocrates, 40
Cassian, 55, 57, 65 f, 68, 76, 78, 81, 83, 86, 88, 90, 97, 101, 109, 113 f, 115, 118, 124, 127 f, 132, 135 f, 147, 152
Celibacy, 22, 27, 39 f, 42–52, 82, 130 f
Cellia, 81, 84 f, 147
Cells, 82, 98 f, 112, 116
Cenobitic monasticism, 15, 76 f, 91–118, 152
Ceres, 26
Chæremon, Bishop of Nilus, 67
Chæremon, the Eremite, 78
Chæremon, the Stoic, 29, 43
Charity, works of, 80, 88, 111, 117, 135
Chenoboskion, 20 f, 80, 92–4
Chiliasm, 60
Christianity, growth of, 36–8
Christian literature, 38–40, 51
Chronius, 69, 88
Chrysostom, 120

Church and monasticism, 128–34
Church government, 40, 60 f
Churches, 83–8, 92, 102, 120, 128, 130
Cleanliness, 122
Clement of Alexandria, 36 f, 39–43, 54
Climate, 30, 66, 69 f
Clysma, 150
Coma, 70
Communication between Churches, 48, 51
Connolly, R. H, 51
Constans, Emperor, 73
Constantine, Emperor, 61, 73, 91
Constantinople, 85
Constantius, Emperor, 73
Contemplativa, De Vita, 34 f.
Contemplative life, 18, 31, 53–7, 68
Conybeare, F C, 23
Coptic versions, 37
Cornelius, 93
Cornutus, 43
Cronius, 43
Crum, W. E, 98
Cumont, F, 26
Cyprian, 50
Cyprus, 142

Daniel, 86
Dead, the, 58 f, 112, 118 f.
Death, 49, 58 f., 65
Delta, 69, 81, 114, 147
Demetrius, 36 f, 60 f.
Denderah, 92
Desert, tendency to the, 66–70
Didache, 36
Diocles, 77
Diognetus, epistle to, 66
Diolcos, 114
Dion Chrysostom, 17
Dionysius, Bishop of Alexandria, 60, 67
Dionysius, Bishop of Milan, 148
Dionysius of Corinth, 48
Dionysius of Rhinocorura, 88
Dioscorus of Nitria, 82
Dioscorus of the Thebaid, 89

Divine worship, 82 f., 102, 115 f.
Dorotheus, a Theban ascetic, 121 f.
Dorotheus of Antinoë, 78
Dorotheus of Athribis, 124
Dracontius, 133
Dress, 101 f , 115
Drummond, J , 34

Economic conditions, 63 f
Education, 103, 125–7
Egypt, condition of, 63–6, 70
Egyptian character, 30, 65
Egyptian Christianity, 36–8
Egyptian Church, circumstances of, 60–3
Elias, 120
Elijah, 77
Ellis, H , 123
Encratites, 39, 41, 51
Encyclopædia Britannica, 13
Encyclopædia of Religion and Ethics, 17, 22, 26, 28, 31, 33, 37, 58, 65, 122 f
Ennathas, 50
Ephesus, Council of, 111
Epiphanius, 36, 45, 142, 148
Episcopal authority, 60 f
Eponymus, 80, 93
Eremites, associations of, 78–90, 149, 152
Eremitical monasticism, 76–8, 112, 118, 152
Erman, A., 29 f , 123
Esneh, 91
Essenes, 22 f.
Etheria, 146
Ethiopia, 16
Eucharist, the, 83, 85, 87, 89, 102, 113–6, 120, 128
Eucheria, 146
Eugenius, 150
Eulalius, 142
Eulogius, 126
Eusebius, 37, 44 f , 48–50, 67
Eusebius, Bishop of Vercelli, 148 f
Eustathius, 142 f.
Eustochium, 145
Evagrius of Antioch, 140
Evagrius Ponticus, 85, 126, 129

Farrar, F W , 70
Fasting, 14, 26, 31, 33, 35, 39, 41, 44, 47 f., 62, 80, 85, 89, 106
Fayum, 28
Férotin, M , 146
Festal letters, 132
Food, 14–16, 32, 35, 44 f , 47, 72, 77 f , 80, 89 f , 98, 105 f , 112, 118
Foreigners, 109
Fronto, 73
Frontonius, 66
Future life, 57–9, 69 f

Galen, 49
Gallienus, 63
Gaul, monasticism of, 149
Gaza, 141
Glover, T. R., 18
Gnosticism, 36, 46–8
Government, monastic, 99 f , 115
Gospel according to the Egyptians, 39
Gospel according to the Hebrews, 36
Gospel of Philip, 47
Great Oasis, 64
Greek influence, 26–32, 43, 48, 53 f
Gregory, 139
Gregory Nazienzen, 57, 131 f , 152
Gregory Thaumaturgus, 45, 143
Grenfell and Hunt, 39, 64
Grutzmacher, G , 20, 91
Gwatkin, H M , 70
Gymnosophists, 16

Hadrian, 28
Hall, H. R , 29
Harnack, *History of Dogma*, 39 f , 46
Harnack, *Mission and Expansion of Christianity*, 37, 49, 61
Harpocrates, 29
Hastings, *Dictionary of Bible*, 33, 122
Heliogobalus, 63
Heliopolis, 31
Hellenistic Judaism, 23, 33–5, 53 f.

Index

Heraclas, 37, 45
Heracleopolis, 68, 70, 88
Hermas, 48
Hermetic literature, 31
Hermopolis Magna, 95, 113
Hermothis, 95
Hero, 128
Heron, 121
Hieracas, 45, 51
Hieroglyphics, 29
Hilarion, 79, 141 f.
Hilgenfeld, A , 14
Historia Lausiaca, 147
Historia Monachorum, 81, 84, 113, 120, 128, 147
Horus, 29

Ignatius, 48
Illness, 106, 135
India, 14-17, 67
Inner mountain, 72, 79
Intermarriage, 29
Isaac, 55
Isaias, 135
Isidore, Bishop of Hermopolis Parva, 82
Isidore of Alexandria, 56, 147
Isidore of the Thebaid, 114
Isidore, priest of Scete, 86
Isis, 30-2, 53 f , 58
Italian monasticism, 147-9

Jacob, 126
Jerome, 22, 41, 66-8, 96-9, 109, 115, 124, 141, 145 f , 148, 152
Jerome's *Regulæ Pachomii*, 96-9
Jerusalem, 85, 145
Jeu, book of, 47
Jews in Egypt, 32-6
John, Abbot, 90, 136
John, a Pachomian monk, 93
John, brother of Pachomius, 93
John of Lycopolis, 77, 125
John of Scete, 87
John of Thmuis, 114
John, the Eremite, 78
Joseph, 78, 125 f.
Josephus, 29
Justin, 38, 49
Juvenal, 32

Kaios, 95
Kapiton, 77 f.
κάτοχοι, 19 f.
Klimax, 86

Labourt, J , 150
Ladeuze, P , 96, 109, 111
Laity, the, 60 f , 70, 128-30
Latopolis, 91, 93 f.
Lausus, 147
Leclerq, H , 151
Leipoldt, J , 111
Leontopolis, 45, 51
Libya, 85, 135
Longinus, 43
Lucius, P E , 23
Lycopolis, 28, 77

Mâ, 26
Macarius of Cellia, 84 f
Macarius of Egypt, 56 f , 79 f., 86
Macarius of Pachnoum, 93
Macarius of Pispir, 68, 80
Macarius, the Alexandrian, 57, 85, 110, 125, 127, 137, 145
Macarius, the younger, 65, 78
Macrina, 143
Magna Mater, 26
Manetho, 29, 31
Mar Awgin, 150
Marcella, 148
Marcionites, 36, 40, 46 f , 51, 92
Marcus of Cellia, 85
Marcus of Memphis, 150 f.
Mareotis, lake, 34
Marmoutiers, 149
Marriage, 22, 27, 39 f , 42-52, 82, 128-30
Martin, 148 f
Martini, Vita, 140 f
Martyrdom, cessation of, 62
Mary, 118 f
Maximin, 73
Melania, 85, 139, 145
Meletians, 92, 133
Melito, 49
Memphis, 15, 19, 26, 88, 140
Men, 119
Mesopotamia, 143 f , 150
Methodius, 49
Milan, 148

Milne, J G., 63 f
Miraculous, the, 137 f., 147
Mithraic cult, 26
Moderatus, 43
Mommsen, T., 33
Monchosis, 80, 93 f
Monasticism and the Church, 128–34
— influence of, 153
— meaning of, 13
— spread of Egyptian, 140–51
Montanism, 37, 47 f, 51
Moses of Calamus, 65, 78
Moses of Scete, 55, 89
Moses, the robber, 65, 86
Mount of Olives, 147
Mummification, 58
Mysticism, 53–7

Narcissus, 49, 66 f.
Nathaniel, 129
Nature, 135–7
Nazarites, 22
Neo-Cynicism, 26
Neo-Platonism, 17 f, 27 f., 54
Neo-Pythagoreanism, 27
Nero, 29
Nesteros, 55, 78, 126
Nikomachus, 43
Nile, 16, 30, 64, 72, 92 f, 95, 104, 111
Nisibis, 150
Nitria, 66, 81–5, 110, 127, 139 f., 145–7, 149
Numbers, 109
Numenius, 43

Obedience, 108, 124, 133
Obi, 95
Or of Nitria, 82
Or of the Thebaid, 88 f.
Origen, 38–40, 43–6, 51 f, 54, 60 f, 83, 143
Origenistic controversy, 139
Orphism, 17, 26
Orsisii, Doctrina, 96
Orsisius, 94–6, 104, 132
Osiris, 29–31, 51, 54, 58
Otto, W., 29
Outer mountain, 72, 79
Oxyrhynchus, 39, 85, 88, 120

Pabau, 93–5, 98, 100, 103 f, 109, 119, 133 f.
Pachnoum, 93, 95
Pachomian rules, development of, 96–9
Pachomian system, 91–110, 114, 127, 135, 147
Pachomii, Vita, 96 f., 104, 109, etc
Pachomius, 20–2, 36, 77, 80, 85, 91–6, 98, 100, 103–6, 108–10, 112 f, 118 f, 123, 125 f, 128–30, 132–5, 138, 144, 148, 150, 152 f.
Pachon, 86, 121, 127
Pæsius, 135
Palæmon, 20 f, 69, 80, 92, 135
Palestine, 23, 50, 66, 79, 139, 141–5
Palladius, 81 f, 84, 86, 88, 96–9, 101 f, 104, 109 f, 119 f, 124, 127, 138, 145–7
Palmyrenes, 63
Pambo, 82, 127, 145
Pamphilus, 50
Panephysis, 78, 114
Panopolis, 93, 104, 110 f, 130
Pantænus, 43, 60
Paphlagonia, 142
Paphnutius (Kephalas), 126
Paphnutius of Heracleopolis, 88
Paphnutius of Scete (possibly = Kephalas), 56, 86 f.
Parousia, 47, 66
Patermucius, 114
Paul, abbot of a cenobitic monastery, 114
Paul, a Pachomian monk, 93
Paul of Mount Pherme, 82
Paul of the Porphyrian Desert, 78, 123 f.
Paul of Thebes, 67 f, 137
Paul the Simple, 79 f, 127
Paula, 145 f, 148
Pauli, Vita, 68
Pavia, 149
Peaceful simplicity of the monastic life and its interruptions, 134–9
Pecusius, 93
Peregrinatio Silviæ, 146

Index

Pergamos, 49
Persecution, 37, 61, 64, 67, 73
Pessimism, 65
Peter, a Pachomian monk, 119
Peter of Eleutheropolis, 50
Petrie, W. M F, 14 f, 22 f., 31
Petronius, 93 f
Philo, 23, 33–5, 53
Philostratus, 27
Phœnice, 88
Photinus, 146
Piamun, 53
Pichnoum, 93
Pierius, 45
Pilgrimages, 138, 141–7
Pinufius, 114
Pior, 123
Pispir, 72 f, 79 f, 84
Pistis Sophia, 36 f., 47
Piteroum, 78
Piterus, 126
Pityrion, 80
Platonism, 41–3
Plotinus, 27 f, 43
Plutarch, 31, 53
Pœmander, 31
Polycarp, 48
Pontitianus, 150
Pontus, 142
Poole, R S, 28
Porphyrian Desert, 78
Porphyry, 28, 43, 54
Posidonius, 78
Postumian, 68, 147
Preuschen, E, 19
Priaulx, O de B, 17
Priscillianism, 151
Probation, 97
Proou, 93
Psentæsis, 93
Pseudo-Clementine epistles, 49
Psois, 93
Ptemencyrcis, 133
Ptolemais, 28, 95
Ptolemy I, 29 f.
Ptolemy of Klimax, 86, 128
Ptolemy Philadelphus, 15
Ptolemy, son of Glaucias, 19
Punishment, 84, 87, 107 f, 113, 117 f
Pythagoreanism, 17, 27, 43, 46

Rechabites, 22
Red Sea, 68, 72
Relations of Pachomian and other monks, 109 f.
Remoboth, 124
Renunciation of the family, 52, 71, 122 f
— of possessions, 33–5, 41, 44 f, 47 f., 50, 52, 71, 124, 151
— of the world, 33–5, 47, 50, 52, 55, 66–9, 124 f
Reuvens, C J. C, 19
Revillout, E, 20
Rhinocorura, 88
Rome, 26, 39, 49, 54, 132, 148, 150
Rufinus, 145–7

Sacrifices of the monks, 121–5
Salamis, 142, 148
Samaria, 49
Samuel, 93
Sarabaites, 124
Sarapion, Bishop of Thmuis, 73, 129
Sarapion of Arsenoitis, 88, 135
Sarapion of Scete, 86
Sarapion the Great, of Nitria, 82, 146
Saturday and Sunday, observance of, 83, 85–7, 102, 112, 115 f, 130
Scete, 79, 81, 85–8, 147
Schaff, P, 63, 75
Schenalolet, 110
Schenesit, 20–2, 80, 92–4
Schenoudi, 110–13, 120, 130, 135, 138
Schmoun, 95
Scott-Moncrieff, P D, 28, 37, 47
Scriptures, the, 35, 37–9, 44, 52 f, 66, 70 f, 83, 85, 87 f, 96 f, 103 f, 114–16, 125–7, 144
Sebaste, 142
Sections, Pachomian, 97 f.
Secularisation of the Church, 61 f
Serapion, see Sarapion
Serapis, 19–22, 28 f., 58, 92
Serenus, 52, 138
Sexual laxity, 123

Silence, 27, 46, 104 f., 118
Silvania, 146
Silvanus, 101
Simeon of Italy, 126
Simon Stylites, 42 f.
Sleep, 28, 44, 72, 88, 90, 97, 106 f.
Smith, V. A., 15
Smyrna, 49
Social and intellectual status of the monks, 125-7
Solomon, 77
Sons of the prophets, 22
Sozomen, 67, 81, 84, 96 f., 122, 142 f., 152
Spain, monasticism of, 146, 151
Spencer, L., 30
Steindorff, G., 65
Stoicism, 26
Suez, 150
Sulpitius, 137, 140, 147
Surus, 93
Syria, 23, 50 f., 62, 142
Syrian Sun God, 26

Tabennesis, 80, 85, 92 f., 95, 100, 132
Taor, 120, 128
Taous, 19
Tase, 93
Teachers, order of, 60 f.
Temouschons, 93
Tentyra, 92, 129
Tertullian, 50, 67
Thaues, 19
Thebeu, 80, 93
Theodore, Abbot, 126 f.
Theodore, disciple of Pachomius, 93-5, 100, 105, 110, 119, 125 f., 132
Theodore of Cellia (probably = Abbot Theodore), 85

Theodore, the Alexandrian, 109, 126
Theodore, the anti-Origenist, 146
Theodosius II, 147
Theon, 126
Theonas, 52, 123
Theophilus, Bishop of Alexandria, 96, 129, 134, 139
Therapeutæ, 22-4, 34 f., 53
Therapeutrides, 35
Thespesion, 16
Thmuis, 114, 125
Timotheus, 31
Timothy, 111
Tismenæ, 93 f., 119
Tollinton, R. B., 42 f.
Troubles of the monks, 138 f.
Turner, C. H., 85
Tyre, Council of 133

Valens, 128
Valentinus, 36
Vercelli, 148 f.
Vespasian, 33
Visitors, 83-5, 88, 90, 97, 99, 108-10, 113 f., 119, 130, 138 f.

Watson, E. W., 138
Weingarten, H., 18, 20, 70
Wendland, P., 23
White Monastery, 110-13
Wine, use of, 27, 31 f., 41, 44 f., 83 f., 106
Women, communities of, 71, 78, 111, 118-20, 145 f.
Work, 14, 23 f., 71-3, 80, 83 f., 87 f., 99 f., 103-5, 116 f., 119, 134 f., 149
Workman, H. B., 152
Worship, Divine, 82 f., 102, 115 f.

www.ingramcontent.com/pod-product-compliance
Lightning Source LLC
Chambersburg PA
CBHW051109160426
43193CB00010B/1370